Writing

D1331625

54 9

T

ONE WEEK LOAN

Writing for Law

Dave Powell
Senior Lecturer in Law
Teesside University

Emma Teare
Senior Lecturer in Law
Teesside University

First published 2010 by
PALGRAVE MACMILLAN

Palgrave Macmillan in the UK is an imprint of Macmillan Publishers Limited,
registered in England, company number 785998, of Houndmills, Basingstoke,
Hampshire RG21 6XS.

Palgrave Macmillan in the US is a division of St Martin's Press LLC,
175 Fifth Avenue, New York, NY 10010.

Palgrave Macmillan is the global academic imprint of the above companies
and has companies and representatives throughout the world.

Palgrave® and Macmillan® are registered trademarks in the United States,
the United Kingdom, Europe and other countries

ISBN 978–0–230–23644–8

This book is printed on paper suitable for recycling and made from fully
managed and sustained forest sources. Logging, pulping and manufacturing
processes are expected to conform to the environmental regulations of the
country of origin.

A catalogue record for this book is available from the British Library.

10   9   8   7   6   5   4   3   2   1
19 18 17 16 15 14 13 12 11 10

Printed by Thomson Litho Ltd, East Kilbride

Contents

Introduction

Why are you doing a law degree? You enjoy it? It will lead to a career in law? It will lead to a career in something else? You drifted into it by accident or for some other reason – or for a mix of them? Whatever the reason, your chances of succeeding will be improved if you improve your grades. And you may surprise yourself; if you do well, your aims may change.

This book aims to improve your grades. It is the result of what we have learned over the years from teaching law students. That is, that the lessons in it work because we have been using them ourselves and have proved it. Students who apply them improve their grades and get better degrees.

Some books of this type set exercises for you to do. We do not. Why not? The answer is that your assignment, exam or other piece of work *is* the exercise. Why do two pieces of work if one can perform two functions? If you use this book from the beginning of your studies you can avoid making the mistakes that arise regularly. If you have already started your course and you have not got the marks you wanted, it will show you why and how to correct the mistakes you have made. Even if you have done well, there is always room for improvement.

The aim is not that you read this book from cover to cover in one go. What we recommend is that you read Part 1, but again not in one go. Take it at the speed that will allow you to absorb what you are reading. Then, when it comes to applying the lessons, you will remember them and be able to go back to them. Subsequent parts of the book, on essays, problem questions and so on, refer back to Part 1, so that is an additional guide. Once you have read Part 1, use the other parts before you start an assessment to which they refer. That way, it will see you through your degree as a help, not a burden. Alternatively, if you have a question about any particular area you can read the relevant chapter in Part 1 and then go to the corresponding place later in the book appropriate to your assessment.

The book is in seven parts. Part 1 is based on a presentation Emma developed as a year tutor on the law degree and which she gives to students. This part contains the general material which is relevant to all types of assessment that you will do. The other parts relate to essays, problem questions, presentations, moots, exams and dissertations; these are all types of assessment which are encountered on undergraduate law degrees. You might use them all but will definitely use some of them. These parts have been developed from materials we have produced over the years, in collaboration with some of our colleagues, for use with our students.

The most important thing about your law course is to have fun. When we say this to our students about doing their exams it always raises a laugh. We are serious. If you enjoy your course and the assessments, it will show. If you are bored when working, the work you do will be dull and boring; if you enjoy what you are doing, the work will be better. We do not promise to remove all the difficult times from your course but we hope that using this book means that there are fewer of them.

We would like to acknowledge the help and assistance of our colleagues at Teesside University who have, over the years, contributed greatly to the ideas which have produced this book. In particular we would also like to thank Professor Ian McLeod, Visiting Professor, Teesside University, for introducing us to the project and for his encouragement to its completion. Our thanks also to Teesside University and Professor Caroline Macdonald, Deputy Vice-Chancellor, for permission to use University copyright materials. At Palgrave Macmillan we would like to thank Suzannah Burywood and Jenni Burnell, our publishers, for the work they have done guiding us through the project. We would like to thank our copy-editor, Caroline Richards, for the expert way in which she has turned our typescript into the book you are now reading. We would also like to record our gratitude to the anonymous reviewers who have commented on this book at various stages in its production and have given us invaluable guidance. Their contributions have improved the final product immeasurably. Any remaining errors are our responsibility.

Dave Powell
Emma Teare

Part 1

Why Should I?

1 The Pragmatic Reason and the More General Reason

By the end of this chapter you should be able to:

► appreciate the function of assessments;
► understand why the skills this book is about are important to you;
► recognise the combination of skills you need.

Passing

You are a law student or a student studying law as part of another course. Although being a student is about many things that are outside the scope of this book, one of the main reasons is that you want to obtain the qualification for which you are enrolled. You can then use it to propel you onto the next stage of your life. This requires that you pass whatever assessments are built into the structure of your course. This book is about passing and then improving further.

Courses which are examined by bodies external to the teaching institution tend to be assessed by examination only. Examples of these include the London External degree and the Institute of Legal Executives qualifications. Where institutions assess their own students, as in universities, assessment is carried out using a variety of methods. In general these are divided into two broad categories, the assignment and the examination.

Assignments take a multitude of forms: there are essays, problem questions, presentations, moots and other forms, but they all have certain things in common. They require you to identify the law relevant to that piece of work, determine what that law is using, statutes, case law and academic authority, criticise that law, again using academic authority, and come to a conclusion. But the most important thing is that in doing this you are able to transmit these things to the people who are marking your work. The aim of this book is to help you to do that.

The value of improving

Once you know how to pass an assignment, the next thing to do is to pass with a good mark. Generally on degree programmes marks contribute to the final degree result from the second year onward. If you have learned how to produce assignments that earn good marks in year 1, it will make it easier to progress to the standards required in year 2 and year 3. And so you will achieve the class of degree you are aiming for. If you only just pass your assignments in year 1, improving to an Upper Second level in year 2 will be much harder. Thus, if you learn the techniques you need to achieve good results in year 1, the effort pays off throughout the course. The outcome will be that the good degree (generally classified as a First or Upper Second) that you want will be within reach. The book will help in years 2 and 3 as well.

Students commonly come to tutors in their final year to tell them that they 'need' an Upper Second (or 2.1), apparently viewing anything less as a failure (which it is not). When they are asked what they have done in the previous two years to work towards that classification, they cannot say. Sometimes the answer is that they have done very little. You are doing something by reading this book. It is hoped that you will take on board the lessons within it. But this is not the only thing you need to draw lessons from. When you receive feedback on your work from your tutors, do not just look at the mark (tempting as this is) and leave it at that. Look at why you have achieved that mark.

The function of coursework

Coursework has two functions. One is to contribute towards your mark for the course. This is called the summative function. It measures achievement and decides which side of the pass/fail boundary your work lies on, and how good or bad a pass or fail it is. The second function, in terms of improving your performance, is more important. It is the formative function: the aim is to enable you to learn both from doing the work and from receiving feedback from the marker. The students referred to above are the ones who have denied the assignments they have done that formative function. They have looked only at the mark and learned very little from it.

But why have we said the formative function is more important? Surely, as we said earlier, the important thing is to pass? It is, but generally on law degrees, if you fail the odd assessment you are given a chance to redo it or to do an alternative one, although normally only for a pass mark. If you learn from an assignment how to do the next one better, not only will you avoid failing, you will progress to higher marks and, we hope, a better class of degree.

● Feedback

So how do you do this? There are three types of feedback. The first, and least useful, is the mark. But saying it is the least useful does not mean it is useless. If it is the only feedback you have been given then you need to know how to use it. This is where the **marking criteria** come in; they may sometimes be called something else but see p. 53. If you have the ones your university uses, use those. If your university does not publish any, use the ones in this book. You will find them in Appendix 1 near the back. You will see that they are divided into Level 1, Level 2 and Level 3. These correspond to the three years on a full-time degree course. Look at the appropriate set of marking criteria and see what they say about work which has a mark in that range. Then look at your work and see what it is about it that makes that description apply. Now look at the criteria for the next classification up. What would make that classification apply to your work rather than the one below? That tells you what you need to do to step up to the next class. How you do that is by applying the lessons from this book. So when your assignment is returned to you, refer to the relevant part of this book to see what you need to do. Some of the terms used in the marking criteria may appear difficult but we will show you what they mean.

The second type of feedback is that contained on a feedback sheet. This will normally be with your work when it is returned. It might be text; it might be completed boxes or some other standard format. What is important about it is that it puts into a narrative form the tutor's views on your work and will, normally, echo the wording of the marking criteria. This enables you to cut out a step of the process for when you have only a mark because you do not have to find what the mark means; your tutor has done it for you. All you now need to do is see why the marker's comments are the ones which apply to your assignment. You can then look at the next classification up from the one you achieved, see what it says and apply it to your work. That makes it sound easy: it is not when you are doing it on your own, but this book will show you how.

The third and best type of feedback is that marked on the work itself. Again, you may not be supplied with this but if you are, use it. It consists of the marker's comments written on your assignment. This enables you to find out not only what you need to do to lift your marks to the next classification but where you need to do it. And the most common word written on assignments is 'why?'. In law it is very easy to tell stories – you have all those wonderful case facts to relate, whether they be about Mrs Carlill or Michael Collins. (Do not worry if you have not heard about them yet; you will.) However, that is not what an assignment should be doing. It should be going into why the principle in a case applies to the question in your assignment. We go into this in detail in Chapter 3.

There is another thing to note about marking criteria. You will see that they demand a higher standard for the same mark as you go through the levels of the programme. Your work needs to be of a higher standard as you move through your degree. This is called 'academic progression' and refers to the process of you gaining in knowledge and your writing style becoming more sophisticated as you progress through your course. Just as you progressed from GCSEs to A-levels or other qualifications, so you progress through your degree. Applying the lessons of this book will help you to do that.

The pragmatic reason

So, in summary, the pragmatic reason for you to apply the lessons we provide are that you will reap a benefit for the amount of effort you put in. If your efforts are misdirected you will not. This benefit is not just a one-off; it will continue throughout your course. This is a pretty good return for reading this book. And it does not stop there.

The academic model

In the past there was a problem. This was that in many instances, organisations running assessments adjusted marks so that a set number of students fitted into each category. This was bad because if one student moved up, it meant another moved down. This happens less now and it should not happen on your degree. There are not fixed proportions of Firsts, 2.1s, 2.2s, Thirds and Fails. In fact, the opposite is now the case. Lecturers love it if you all do well so you will be given the marks you deserve. But you have to earn them.

It is called maintaining academic standards. Your marks should say something about you. That is why we use marking criteria. They help to point to things in the piece of work and say why it is worth a particular mark. That means a mark does not, or it should not, depend on who has marked it. You often hear critics, particularly newspaper columnists and politicians, complaining that qualifications are being 'dumbed down'. We do not want anyone being able to say that about a law degree. It matters to us.

It matters to you as well because you would be the first to suffer if degrees were handed out to people who had not earned them. Equally, if your degree classification did not reflect your ability, why would your future employer put any faith in it? By ensuring you achieve what you have earned we can give them that assurance. And employers appreciate it. They tell us regularly. That benefits you.

Skills

You can achieve that good degree by following the fairly simple rules which are contained in this book. How? Many people think of a degree as meaning you have a certain amount of knowledge. Whilst this is important, it is also important that you have skills. On a law degree, two skills are particularly important. One is learning how to learn. The law you learn on your degree becomes out of date quite quickly. Law changes very fast (and very unevenly). By learning how to find out what the law is, you can make sure that you can access the current law on any topic that you need.

The second important skill is to be able to communicate what you know to someone else. You could be the world's greatest genius but if you cannot transmit what you understand to anyone else, who would know? There is no point in talking into your mobile if no one is listening. There is no point in your understanding an area of law on your degree unless you can transmit that understanding to the people who are assessing you.

These two skills are what this book is about. You do not do well in assessments by parroting back to your lecturers what they have told you. And you do not do well in assessments if your lecturers cannot understand what you are trying to tell them. We aim to enable you to give your lecturers what they are looking for in a way they can understand. That will earn you good marks.

Another reason that this development matters to you is that university is practice for real life. Your degree course gives you the chance to make mistakes, learn how to put them right, and then to build on that. This is the 'academic progression' we referred to earlier. In your future career the first time is for real. If you do something seriously wrong, you may not be able to put it right later. And even if you can, people will remember the mistake rather than you putting it right.

It does not matter if you are planning to join the legal profession as a solicitor, barrister or legal executive, or if you plan to do some other form of legal work or something outside of law altogether. The skills you acquire on a law degree are highly sought after. If you do well, you will be very marketable. You may also surprise yourself. We have lost count of the number of students who have told us they did not want to enter the legal profession and who, some time later, have come back to us for a reference because they were doing just that. In fact, neither of us did our law degrees intending to be law lecturers.

But if you can demonstrate that you have these skills and can practise them at a high level, then you will have opportunities to do many things. You just decide what suits you best. If you cannot demonstrate these skills, your opportunities will be more limited.

Summary

This chapter has explained why you might use this book:

- to pass the course;
- to contribute to final marks and so improve your degree result;
- to use the feedback on your work to improve your results as the standard required increases as you progress through the course;
- to ensure you achieve what you deserve and by following some fairly simple rules that can be what leads to a good degree.

2 Why Do Students Fail?

Answering the question

Why do students fail? You would think this would be obvious! Students fail because they do not know enough, they do not do enough work or they do not submit work when it is due. All these are reasons why students fail – but they are not the only ones. The surprising reason why many students fail is that they do not answer the question that has been set; they answer a related one. This is very easy to do, not only in exams but in assignments as well. Why? Because if you are fairly confident about something, it is very easy to convince yourself that the question is about that rather than about something you are less confident about.

So how does this come about? The notes your lecturers have given you will have looked at the area of law to be covered by your assignment or exam question in a particular way. You will also find that textbooks and journal articles will do the same, and that they will frequently tackle something in ways that are very similar to each other. This is because there are conventions in the academic study of the various areas of law which most academics follow. It is very easy to imagine that your assignment or exam question is asking you to follow one of these paths. That is true rarely. If you have convinced yourself of this, what you will do is reproduce what you have done in lectures or what you have read and that will not be an answer to the question. Academics tend not to set questions which ask you to reproduce your notes on a particular topic. So do not do it.

It is also very easy to convince yourself that what is required to answer a question is the history of how a particular area of law developed to where it is today because you can find that easily in textbooks. However, the course you are doing is a law course, not a history one, so what is important is what the law now is, not how it came to be so. This is a very easy trap to fall into because of the way the common law works by being developed from, apparently, fixed sets of principles over long periods of time. We use the word 'apparently' because, as you will come to learn, there are occasionally shocks to the system where the learning of centuries is suddenly re-evaluated; then it turns out that the principles on which some areas of law are based are very different from what has been accepted until then. So, for example, if your question is about equitable principles and why they are needed, do not write about the fusion of law and **equity**. What you have been asked about is the place of equity in law today.

If it is this easy to slip into doing your assignment or exam question wrong, and so failing or at least getting a much lower mark than you would expect, how can you avoid this problem? There are three things you need. The first and most obvious is the question that has been set. This needs to be at the centre of your answer, so make sure that when you are writing, the question is always in vision. Do not assume you know what the assignment or exam question is asking and therefore put the question to one side. As we will see, this is particularly important in answering questions in examinations when you do not have the luxury of revising what you have written.

There are two other things that are important besides the question and you may not have come across them before. The first is the **learning outcomes**. They may be called something different in your university but they are recognisable in that they tell students what is being assessed in any particular piece of work, in the subject and in the degree overall. In many universities these are provided with the assignment; in others they are contained in the handbook for the course. Make sure you know what they are and keep those in focus. In case your university does not publish the learning outcomes for particular assessments, some fairly typical ones are provided in Appendix 2 (p. 198), at the back of this book.

The other thing you need to bear in mind are the **marking criteria** which are being used. They may go by other names such as 'standards' but what they do is the same: they indicate, for each level on a programme, what the work needs to be to achieve a particular grade. Again, most universities provide their students with marking criteria and if you have them, use those. If you do not have them from your university you will find a set of fairly typical marking criteria in the appendix of this book. The marking criteria provide a description of how markers place assessments into a particular class. In addition to the general marking criteria, for some types of assessment – notably those which involve some element of presentation such as an oral presentation, a moot or a poster presentation – there are also likely to be marking criteria specifically for that activity. If you are doing one of these types of assessment, find out what they are and use them. In case your university does not publish these there are a set in Appendix 1 (p. 188).

Once the necessary materials are assembled you are in a position to work out what the question you have been set is asking and what your tutors are looking for as an answer. This will be examined in more detail in the later parts of this book since the answers vary according to the different types of assessment: essays are looking for one thing (p. 71), problem questions for something else (p. 95) and so on with other assessments.

Relevance

One problem common to many types of assessment is a loss of relevance. The work will start appropriately but then the marker will come across a sentence, a paragraph, a page or perhaps even several pages with no obvious relevance to what the student is supposed to be doing. This problem is fairly easy to solve even in the stress of an examination.

A paragraph should contain a discrete element of your answer and is the easiest level at which to tackle the problem. When you have written a paragraph, stop. Then read that paragraph back to yourself and ask yourself, 'What does this paragraph do to answer the question?' If the answer is 'nothing', there are two possible reasons.

One of them is that what you have written is rubbish which has nothing to do with the question – and so the paragraph should be deleted. However, this is unlikely, especially if you have followed the lessons of this book.

The more likely answer is that there is a connection between what you have written and the question in your head; it has just not made it as far as the paper or the computer screen. This can normally be corrected with the addition of a sentence at the end of the paragraph pointing out that connection. The marker can only mark what is in front of them, not what is in your head. By making this addition you have shown not only that you can identify relevant points and discuss them but can identify how those points are relevant to the question and specify this relevance.

The key concept

What do the two things covered in this chapter have in common? They are about answering the question. One way to ensure that you are both answering the right question and maintaining relevance is for the wording of the question to repeat throughout your answer. It is like reading 'Blackpool' through a stick of rock. No matter where a marker bites into your answer they will find the question. Obviously, how you do this varies with the type of assessment and it will be examined in each as appropriate, but the general rule is that if you use the exact words that form the question in demonstrating the relevance of your answer you will retain that relevance. Retain the relevance and you will be answering the correct question appropriately and, as a result, gaining the marks that will start you on the path to a good degree and all the possibilities that brings.

Summary

This chapter has looked at:

- the reason why students fail assessments for technical reasons;
- the twin faults of not answering the right question and failing to retain relevance;
- strategies for avoiding these problems using the question, learning outcomes and marking criteria.

3 Description v. Analysis

By the end of this chapter you should be able to:

▶ understand that assessments are about 'why' not 'what';
▶ appreciate the value of relevance in your work;
▶ recognise legal authority and be able to use it.

Telling stories

Demonstrating a principle without telling a story is one of the harder skills to grasp. In law it is very easy to tell stories. After all, you have all those wonderful case facts to play with, so why not use them? You do use them; the case is your authority and, as we said earlier, a law assignment is nothing without authority. Here is an example of what is seen frequently:

Example

In the case of *Carlill v Carbolic Smoke Ball Co.* [1893] 1QB 256 the company issued an advert offering to pay £100 to anyone who used their smoke ball according to the instructions and later got flu. Mrs Carlill bought a smoke ball and used it as prescribed but got flu. She sued for the £100 and won.

So what is wrong with that? Factually it is correct but what it is telling the reader is *what* happened, not *why*. As a result, it will not help your assignment. What you need to use authority for is to demonstrate why the legal position is as it is. How do you do that? You use the case to demonstrate a principle, or several principles, instead of telling the story. Most of the time you do not need the detailed facts; what you need is the 'why', and here is an example:

Improved answer

In the case of *Carlill v Carbolic Smoke Ball Co.* [1893] 1QB 256 the Court of Appeal held that the advert issued by the company was a unilateral offer and that Mrs Carlill accepted it by fulfilling its terms. As Bowen LJ said:

> Although the offer is made to the whole world, the contract is made with that limited portion of the public who come forward and perform the condition on the faith of the advertisement.
>
> As a result, a person who advertises something may be making such an offer.

What you are explaining now is *why*. You have established the principle set by this case and so can go on to use it to continue your discussion. We will look at how you do this in different types of assignment later in the book but this is the basis of establishing authority. Can you see the difference between this example and the one above? These are not extreme examples; they are what law lecturers see all the time. The first example leads you nowhere because it establishes nothing. The second leads you somewhere, to a set of principles to be applied.

Here is another example:

Example

> In *Donoghue v Stevenson* [1932] AC 562 the court decided that the manufacturer of the ginger beer could be liable for there being a snail in the bottle.

Again, factually this is correct. However, it tells you nothing, beyond the bare facts, and leads you nowhere. It is all 'what' and no 'why'. As a result, it is of no use in your assignment. If you leave it like that the marker is entitled to say 'So what?' or 'What is your point?'. Here it is again:

Improved answer

In *Donoghue v Stevenson* [1932] AC 562 Lord Atkin in the House of Lords established the neighbour principle as the basis for a duty of care to arise in tort. In response to the question in law as to who is my neighbour, he said at p. 619:

> The answer seems to be – persons who are so closely and directly affected by my act that I ought reasonably to have them in contemplation as being so affected when I am directing my mind to the acts or omissions which are called into question.

Again, you have now answered why, not just what. You have both said what the principle is and explained the basis of how it works. You have established authority for what you are saying and provided the platform to use this authority to take your assignment further. If the assignment is an essay on the duty of care in negligence, you can then follow the various refinements of these principles which have been developed in subsequent cases; if you are addressing a problem question on the liability of a manufacturer to the user of a product, you can do so directly. Whichever of these assignments you are tackling, you have set yourself on a path that will lead to a good piece of work.

Similarly, if you are producing an assignment on the subject of homicide by omission you might say:

Example

> In *Airedale NHS Trust v Bland* [1993] AC 789 it was decided that doctors would not be guilty of murder if they stopped feeding Tony Bland, who was in a persistent vegetative state.

But the problem is, this is all 'what'. It tells you what the result of the case was but leads nowhere and so does not help in a line of argument, which is what your assignment ought to be about. The version here is a dead end, whereas what you are looking for is what will lead on to the next part of the assignment. To do that you need the principle, so the same idea might become:

Improved answer

In *Airedale NHS Trust v Bland* [1993] AC 789 the House of Lords held that the doctors treating Tony Bland would not be guilty of murder if they stopped feeding him even though the result would be that he would die. This was because he had no interest in being kept alive so they had no duty to continue treating him. Where there is no duty there can be no crime by omission.

Now you have said 'why'. In cases of homicide by omission – homicide includes both murder and manslaughter – there can only be a conviction where the person accused of the crime owes the victim a duty to act. Once the duty to act does not exist, as in this case, there can be no conviction.

Again, this leads somewhere. If you are writing an essay on liability for omissions in the criminal law, it has given you the basis on which to build. If you are answering a problem question on homicide by omission you can use the example directly, applying it to the scenario you have been given.

● Relevance

In the previous chapter we discussed relevance: why is what you have said included in your assignment? This is important here because lecturers frequently come across things in assignments that leave them puzzled because they appear to bear no relation to what is being discussed. One example we had was:

> **Example**
>
> The European Commission consists of 27 members.

This is perfectly correct but why would such a statement be relevant to your assignment? The response of the marker would be 'and ...?' On its own it is not relevant at all and so should not be in the assignment. If it is to be relevant you need to say why it is relevant. Bald statements of fact like these generally are not.

Now let us take this a little further. Doing a piece of work on judicial precedent, you might want to say:

> **Example**
>
> Judges follow decisions in earlier cases, subject to some exceptions, even when these are not binding on them. The reason for this is that it brings certainty to the law so that a lawyer advising someone about their legal position can be reasonably certain that the advice will be correct.

This is true and you could not be faulted for saying it. However, if you also demonstrate what you are saying it gives the statement more emphasis and so is likely to produce a better result. This could be:

Improved answer

Judges follow decisions in earlier cases, subject to some exceptions, even when these are not binding on them. As Lord Scarman said in *Gillick v West Norfolk and Wisbech Area Health Authority* [1985] 3 WLR 830 (HL) 855:

> The underlying principle of the law was exposed by Blackstone and can be seen to have been acknowledged in the case law. It is that parental right yields to the child's right to make his own decisions when he reaches a sufficient understanding and intelligence to be capable of making up his own mind on the matter requiring decision.

This brings a measure of certainty to the law and enables a lawyer advising someone about their legal position to be reasonably certain that the advice will be correct.

What you have done is to show Lord Scarman using this principle to arrive at his decision in this case. It is no longer just a statement of fact but one which has been demonstrated to be true. You have not only said why but you have also given authority to support your statement. This is an important point in academic work in general and in law in particular. Although the argument is your own, it must be backed up by authority. This authority might be an Act of Parliament, a judgment in a leading case or an academic opinion from a textbook or journal article.

So far we have only used extracts from judgments but when using, for example, a journal article as authority for an argument the process is very similar. If you were doing an essay on the European Court of Justice you might say:

Example

> The ECJ used the rule of reason to expand the scope of the free movement of goods under Article 28 in *Cassis de Dijon*.

Again, this is correct – but by using academic authority, rather than what could be seen as your own opinion, you make a better case. This might become:

> **Improved answer**
>
> As Smith explains, the ECJ used the rule of reason to expand the
> scope of the free movement of goods under Article 28 in *Cassis de
> Dijon*.

You then reference the journal article as a footnote or endnote depending on
the instructions for the assignment. Referencing is covered in Chapter 5 (pp.
38–52). The author you have cited and referenced provides the authority for
what you have said and this will give a better mark than the plain statement.
You have strengthened the academic weight of your statement by using
authority.

Authority

So what is authority? It can be divided roughly into fact and opinion and the
way you use them is different although it produces the same result. Facts
can be said to come from primary sources and opinion from secondary
ones.

Primary sources in law are Acts of Parliament (statutes) and other legislative materials and cases. These are their own authority and you should not
reference the content of an Act or judgment to a textbook or journal article,
as is frequently done. For example, if you are doing a piece of work on theft
you might say:

Example 1: using an Act

> The Theft Act 1968 s 1(1) provides that there is only an offence
> of theft when the perpetrator acts dishonestly.

This needs no further support. You have stated one of the provisions and that
is sufficient. An alternative way of doing this is to quote the provision
directly. This might be:

Example 2: using an Act

The Theft Act 1968s 1(1) states that:

> A person is guilty of theft if he dishonestly appropriates the property belonging to another ...

In the first example you cited the requirement indirectly; in the second you cited it directly by quoting from the Act. Neither requires further authority.

Similarly, if you are using a judgment as your authority, the content of that judgment is sufficient. Looking at the principles relating to the judicial review of administrative action, you might say:

Example 1: using a judgment

Lord Denning held in *R v Barnsley Metropolitan District Council, ex parte Hook* that it was contrary to the rules of natural justice for a person to give evidence to a committee and to be present whilst the committee discussed the decision to be made.

This needs no further support and it would be wrong to reference this statement to a textbook or journal article. As before, an alternative – and perhaps stronger – approach might be to use a direct quote:

Example 2: using a judgment

Lord Denning stated in *R v Barnsley Metropolitan District Council, ex parte Hook* that:

> It is contrary to natural justice that one who is in the position of a prosecutor should be present at the deliberations of the adjudicating committee.

The authority is in the quotation and it needs no more. We would penalise a student who referenced this to a secondary source, a textbook or journal article, as the primary source, the case report, is better authority. However, we must stress that this view is not held by all lecturers and some would not penalise such a reference.

Academic authority

What you do need academic authority for is comment. The last thing a marker wants to see on an undergraduate assessment is 'I think' or 'I believe'. Academic tradition in general, and academic tradition in law in particular, works on citation: that is, using the writings of academics to support an opinion. For example, lecturers frequently see something like this:

Example

> The Court of Appeal was in error in the case of *Re A (Children)* because it was held that the operation to separate the conjoined twins, Jodie and Mary, was permissible even though the operation was not in the best interest of Mary.

Although this is a perfectly defensible academic position it will gain little credit because it is not backed by authority. There are several ways this could be corrected. One might be:

Improved answer 1

Some academic opinion holds that the Court of Appeal was in error in the case of *Re A (Children)* because it was held that the operation to separate the conjoined twins, Jodie and Mary, was permissible even though the operation was not in the best interest of Mary.

You would then reference the statement to a passage in a book or journal article in which the author expressed that opinion. You have now provided authority for your statement and so will gain credit for it in the marking. You paraphrased the author's statement – that is, you provided the sense of it – but in your own words. Alternatively you could say:

Improved answer 2

Powell in his article states that the Court of Appeal was in error in the case of *Re A (Children)* because it was held that the operation to separate the conjoined twins, Jodie and Mary, was permissible even though the operation was not in the best interest of Mary.

You then reference the article to which you have referred. Again, you have provided the marker with the authority for your statement, also by paraphrasing it, and so will be credited for what you have written. Another possibility is:

Improved answer 3

It has been said that:

> the Court of Appeal was in error in the case of Re A (Children) because it was held that the operation to separate the conjoined twins, Jodie and Mary, was permissible even though the operation was not in the best interest of Mary.

Then you reference the quotation to the book or journal article. Instead of paraphrasing, as in the previous two examples, you have now quoted the author directly. Another way of doing the same thing is:

Improved answer 4

Powell stated in his article that:

> the Court of Appeal was in error in the case of Re A (Children) because it was held that the operation to separate the conjoined twins, Jodie and Mary, was permissible even though the operation was not in the best interest of Mary.

Again, reference the article quoted.

All these forms of using authority are acceptable and are equally creditworthy. Which of them you use is up to you. We would advise that, in general, you use a mixture of them so that your assignment is not dominated by one form of citation. It is quite common for lecturers to see student assignments which are a collection of quotations that do not appear to be going anywhere. Using a mixture of direct quotation and paraphrasing can be useful in maintaining the direction you want your assignment to follow. There are exceptions to this rule but we will come to those later.

Fact v. opinion

We said earlier that authority can be divided roughly into fact and opinion and the way you use them is different although it produces the same result. Facts can be said to come from primary sources and opinion from secondary ones. As you will find throughout your studies in law, virtually every statement is subsequently qualified. 'However' must be one of the most frequently used words on law courses.

We need to qualify what we said because not everything in a judgment can be labelled as fact; some of it is opinion. There are two principal reasons for this: one is that in **appellate courts** and some others there is more than one judge. If judges agree on the outcome of the case but differ in their reasons for coming to that conclusion then these differences in reasoning are opinion rather than fixed law. Additionally, a judge may disagree on the result but be outvoted by the other judges and so will have provided a **dissenting judgment**. The other reason is that, as you will learn fairly early in your study of law, judicial decisions are divided into the *ratio decidendi*, the reason for the decision, and *obiter dicta*, things said by the way which are not essential in reaching the decision. The *ratio* is the binding part of the decision, that is, what the law is; the *obiter dicta* are not binding but courts will take notice of them. They can be characterised as opinion.

As a result, you can use judicial opinion in the same way as you use academic opinion to provide authority for what you are saying. An example of using different reasons given by judges for their decision might be:

Example: judicial opinion

In *Re R* Lord Donaldson likened consent to medical treatment to a key. As a result anyone who had the power to consent had a key and any one key was sufficient consent.

Neither of the other judges reasoned the decision in this way but all agreed on the result, so Lord Donaldson's analogy is opinion, albeit a powerful one. What it gives you is the authority for a line of discussion. A dissenting judgment can do the same. For example:

Example: dissenting judgment

Roch LJ in *R v Canons Park Mental Health Review Tribunal, ex parte A* considered that, although the section did not state that the patient had to be treatable to be refused a discharge from detention under the Mental Health Act 1983, this was implied in the wording. The other judges disagreed.

This again provides authority for an argument, even though it is not a statement of the law because the *ratio* of the case was to the opposite effect. An example of something said *obiter* might be:

Example: *obiter* statement

The House of Lords in *Hedley, Byrne & Co. Ltd. v Heller & Partners* considered that there could only be a duty of care in relation to economic loss if there was a special relationship between the parties. Although this statement was *obiter* as it was held that the exclusion clause in the contract was effective, it has been the basis of decisions on economic loss ever since.

Once more, you have used the authority of the case even though this part of what was said was not necessary to the eventual decision so was not part of the *ratio*.

Summary

In this chapter we have discussed:

- description versus analysis and authority;
- 'why' not 'what';
- why you should be wary of including detailed case facts;
- why authority is important to support what you have said;
- the types of authority: from a statute, a judgment, a textbook, a journal article or another source;
- the way authority is used.

4 Sources

By the end of this chapter you should be able to:

▶ identify legal authority;
▶ distinguish between primary and secondary sources;
▶ access those sources;
▶ appreciate some problems with authority.

Authority

In the last chapter we looked at authority and how you need to use it to support your work. This chapter is about where you find your authority and how to judge whether a source is authoritative or not.

The easiest option is that if your lecturers give you materials, be they cases, extracts from textbooks, journal articles or other sources, you can be fairly certain that these are of sufficient authority. After all, your lecturers want you to succeed so they are not going to mislead you. Even here, though, you need to be careful. Lecture notes from your tutors are not authoritative because they have not been through the processes that are necessary for them to be so and so you should not cite them, although they will be useful in pointing you towards other sources, textbooks and journal articles, which are what you need. There is another problem with lecturers providing the materials to students, a problem which is seen repeatedly. When these students, some of whom have been provided with their materials through the whole of their degree courses, go on to other things such as **professional courses** to qualify as solicitors or barristers or study at Master's level, they can sometimes become lost. On these courses they will not be given the materials. They will have to find them and if they have not learned how to do so they are at a disadvantage.

Research

So how do you find things for yourself? Again, your tutors will have helped you by providing reading lists. These will include textbooks and journal articles which they have chosen because they believe that these are the sources that will be of most use to you. These are your starting point.

When you are given your assignment, re-read the relevant part of the textbook recommended for your course. Why re-read? It is hoped that you have already read it to accompany the lecture and seminar on the topic. (If you have not been in the habit of doing so, start now.) At first this may seem like a great deal of reading. However, you will find that once you get into the habit it is not that onerous. You might even enjoy it.

So, to go back to your assignment: the textbook together with your lecture and seminar notes will provide the basic information you need to begin to structure what you are going to do. Your tutors may also have provided materials for you on your **VLE** (Virtual Learning Environment) so you can access these as well. These sources will also, in turn, provide you with further sources: other textbooks, legislation, cases, journal articles and other materials which they cite. These will be the building blocks for your assignment and although different types of assignment either use different building blocks or the same ones but in a different way (which we will see later), these are the basics. Once they are in place and you know how to use them, you can move on to further developments. Get the basics right and moving on from there is easy; get the basics wrong and you are storing up difficulties for yourself later.

You may be asking yourself a question here. Surely, most of this material is available online and so all I have to do is access it that way? It is true that much of the material is available online but some is not. Not all textbooks have online versions and those which do are generally support materials, unless you pay to access the book itself. More importantly, you need to learn to use text-based material. Why? The answer, as it often does, comes down to money.

Many of the best online resources, which you can access free whilst you are at university, are not free; they are provided by companies who trade in the information marketplace. You have free access to them because your university has paid for you to have it. The companies in turn have enabled your university to provide you with access at a reduced cost. They know that if they charged the full commercial rate universities would not be able to afford it and so the material would not be available to you. Obviously this helps you because the material is very useful and tracking it down without this resource is more time-consuming and difficult than doing it online. After all, your library probably only has one paper copy of the various journals, so if you and your colleagues on the course are all trying to use the same one, it can be difficult. However, the companies marketing online resources are commercial organisations; they have to make a profit to stay in business and develop their materials. In many instances they do this by charging commercial users, such as solicitors' firms or barristers' chambers, not only a subscription fee similar to the one a university pays but also a fee for each search. This cost then has to be either passed on to the client or absorbed. Either way, it is an expense. Yet the firm or chambers will have at least the basic paper resources. You will be expected to use these rather than accessing expensive online material. If you do not know how to do it you are (at the least) of less use to the firm or chambers and potentially even a liability. We have heard of new recruits costing firms large sums of money because they have used the online material in the same way they did at university. So by all means access journals and other materials online but make sure you can use the paper versions too.

Quality

The other thing that needs to be discussed here is quality. We talked earlier about authoritative sources – but how does a source become authoritative? Legislation and case law are authority in themselves; the former is the law and the latter judicial interpretation of it. These are primary sources. Other materials, secondary sources, become authoritative because of the processes they go through. Textbooks are commissioned by publishers from experienced academics and go through a rigorous approval process, being reviewed at stages by other academics, which thus ensures their quality. Journal articles are submitted by academics and practitioners to editors who have them reviewed by other academics and practitioners before agreeing to their publication. This again ensures quality. Some errors do get through this process but in general you can assume a textbook or journal article has been through a quality control process and so can be cited with reasonable confidence.

The same is not true about other possible sources so you need to be wary of these. This is particularly so of internet sources. It is very easy for material to be posted on the internet, either on someone's own site or on open access sites. The problem is that these have little or no quality control, so what you find may be good – but, conversely, it may be poor and frequently is. That is why universities pay for you to have access to the specialist law databases: they can be sure the material is of sufficient quality for you to use with confidence. Use these rather than open access materials. If you write something which is wrong, based on an open access source, your tutors will not be impressed by the defence that you found it on the internet.

Authoritative sources

So what are these specialist law databases? They fall into two basic categories: those provided by non-profit organisations as academic resources and those provided by commercial organisations.

The first category, non-profit organisations, are varied but the two cited most frequently in this book are the British and Irish Legal Information

Institute (BAILII), which is available at www.bailii.org, and the UK Centre for Legal Education (UKCLE) at www.ukcle.ac.uk. The former is useful for cases and statutes as well as other source material, and the latter for materials relating to legal education. Others which are useful are those of official bodies such as the Government's statute and statutory instrument database, the Supreme Court and the Law Commission. Details of these are given when the relevant material is being discussed.

Examples of commercial databases are Lexis Library and Westlaw UK but there are others too, and what is available to you will depend on what services your university subscribes to. What they do is provide access to cases, statutory materials, journal articles and other resources by means of searches using various search mechanisms. As these types of database all have different mechanisms – although they have much in common with each other – you will be taught how to use them and the organisations themselves provide easily useable teaching materials to subscribing universities. Make sure you receive them when they are being distributed because you will find them invaluable for your course.

Why are these sources authoritative and others not? The non-profit ones are produced by academics and so have gone through the formal publishing processes or are primary sources made easily available. The commercial sources are mostly primary and secondary source material from elsewhere, case reports and journal articles, and so they have also been through formal processes. Where these commercial organisations produce specialist materials for their sites they use the same processes, so you can rely on their materials.

Non-authoritative sources

Caution also needs to be exercised in citing newspapers or magazines as sources. There are two basic reasons for this. The first is the same as the internet one: where is the quality control? These are not specialist materials written by lawyers for lawyers; they are written by journalists for the general public, or at least that part of it which is their readership. One example was:

> **Company Prosecuted for Mis-selling**
> It was announced today that Xxx was being sued by customers to whom it mis-sold securities.

Here the text of the article was right – customers were suing the company, that is they were claiming damages for their losses in the civil courts – but the headline was wrong because when someone is prosecuted they are accused of a crime and are therefore before criminal courts.

Newspaper articles are also normally written in a hurry to meet a deadline and so lack the checking processes which would help ensure accuracy. Journalists are often not specialists in the area they cover so that even the quality newspapers not only get things wrong but get the same things wrong repeatedly. For example:

> ... the Human Rights Act, based on EU legislation, ...

is something you can find in a newspaper article most days of the week. It is wrong. The Human Rights Act is based on the European Convention on Human Rights, which was developed by the Council of Europe, a body separate and distinct from the EU. The newspaper which published this did correct it, but shortly after it contained something like this:

> The House of Lords debate highlighted two areas in which the EU has stepped into the gaping hole left by the UK government. In December, the European Court of Human Rights ruled that retaining the DNA of the innocent breached article eight of the human rights convention.

This despite the newspaper's instructions to its writers being to the effect that: *The European Court of Human Rights has nothing to do with the EU: it is a Council of Europe body.* There are many other common errors, which, if you copy them, will be marked as wrong.

The second basic reason for caution is that newspapers and magazines generally have a political agenda. This might not necessarily mean that they support any particular political party (although they may do), but that they will frequently slant their coverage to push a specific line. This can lead them to misrepresent or exaggerate. For example, a statement which appears in newspapers regularly is:

> A prisoner has used the Human Rights Act to enforce his right to pornography in prison.

This statement is false. It is true that a person serving a prison sentence tried to apply for a ruling that denying him pornography in prison was a breach of his human rights – but the application was thrown out. As a result of these twin problems the advice we would give in relation to using newspapers as sources is: do not do it.

● Primary sources

As we said before, sources can be divided into primary sources and secondary sources. Primary sources are legislation and cases; secondary sources are everything else.

Finding an Act of Parliament is easy; in fact there are so many ways of doing it that it is often difficult to decide which one to use. As far as paper sources go, your university library almost certainly subscribes to at least one of the main editions, such as the Public General Acts and Law Reports Statutes. These are published in year volumes, now several volumes a year, so to look up an Act, find the year and go to the index. All volumes will have the full index for the year so you do not need to go through them all. The index will give you the volume number, if applicable, and page. To find the text of an Act online is easy and free. Go to the Office of Public Sector Information website, which is part of the national archive, at www.opsi.gov.uk/acts.htm and you will find all Public General Acts since 1988 and a more limited selection back to 1837. The material on the site is subject to Crown copyright protection but it may be used free (see the Crown Copyright Notice on the site).

However (that word again), what these sources will give you is the original text of the Act. For a new piece of legislation that probably will not be a problem. For older legislation it may be that the Act has been amended by subsequent legislation, and it is not unknown for Acts to be amended by other Acts passed in the following year or two. The sources given above will not tell you that. For that you need other sources. Your library will almost certainly have a set of Halsbury's Statutes, which come with an updating service. These are very useful for items you are not going to use very much but they suffer the defect of all publishing: by the time something is published it is out of date. For legislation you are going to use frequently it is often worth buying a book of statutes on the relevant area. A number of publishers produce them and they tend to be updated every year.

Obviously it is easier for online suppliers to update their materials and so that may be a better source for the current text of legislation. The law databases provided by your university will give you the up-to-date text of any legislation – or there are free sources. One useful one is the British and Irish Legal Information Institute at www.bailii.org, which contains a legislation database.

It is difficult to go further as the answers will depend on what your library has, although there is guidance to universities which most follow. Your library should have an information sheet, generally now available online, on what sources are available to you and how you find them. If your library does not, many university libraries have them freely available. You access them by going to the university website – libraries are usually listed under departments – and go to information sources or factsheets. You will be asked for a subject area, generally on a drop-down menu; select law and this should give you a list of what is available. Click on the relevant one and it should come up in one of the major online formats.

Cases are easier since the outcome in an individual case does not change once appeals are exhausted. Again, make sure you can access the paper sources. Your university will have a number of different sets. When you get a case you will see that it frequently has several references after it. Choose one and track that down. All libraries should at least have the Incorporated Council Law Reports and the All England Law Reports. The reference – and if you have not got one just look the case up in a textbook and that will give you one – will be to a set of law reports, a year, possibly a volume, and a page. Again, your library should have factsheets with the main reports listed with their citation so you can find out what they are. We have provided you with a basic list in Appendix 3 (p. 204), at the back of this book.

Online sources are very easy but remember what we said earlier about cost and make sure you know how to access the paper sources. The law databases your university subscribes to on your behalf have the major series going a long way back. You merely put the case name into the case search and it will find it for you. For more recent cases there are free sources. Supreme Court cases from 2009 are available from the Supreme Court website at www.supremecourt.gov.uk. House of Lords cases are available from the website at www.publications.parliament.uk/pa/ld/ldjudgmt.htm from 1996 to 2009, and an extensive number of cases are available on the British and Irish Legal Information Institute site at www.bailii.org listed by jurisdiction, court and year. This explosion of online availability has had an effect on case citation. Cases now have neutral citations – that is, citations which stay the same no matter where the case is published as well as the citations for the major series of law reports. Details of these neutral citations can also be found in Appendix 3 (p. 204).

● **Secondary sources**

As far as secondary sources go, we have already said that your tutors will have directed you to recommended textbooks. Use them. However, as you progress through your study of law you will be expected to widen your sphere of reference beyond statutes, case reports and textbooks. One of the most important areas you will be expected to refer to, particularly for essays and dissertations, is journal articles. Using these used to be hard work as they had to be tracked using paper indices and it was likely that a library would have only one paper copy – if a whole cohort of students was trying to use the same one it was impossible, so lecturers started providing them. Nowadays this should not be necessary; this is where your specialist law databases are invaluable. By typing into the journal search facility the appropriate search terms you will get a list of journal articles which meet those terms. You can browse through the list to decide which of them will be of most use to you and concentrate on those.

An important skill to learn here is how to construct your search terms. If there is one leading case that is fairly recent, using that as a search term can be useful. What *not* to do is use much older cases without any refinement in searching because you will get an immense list which is far too much to sift through. For example:

Scenario

Your assignment is about consideration in contract where the parties already have a contract but agree extra payment without any extra duties. You know from the notes your lecturer gave you that the leading case is *Stilk v Myrick* from 1809. Put that into a journal search and you will get hundreds if not thousands of results. There are two options here. One is to narrow the search by asking only for articles from, say, the last 3 years; another is to narrow it by adding a second, more recent case, in this instance perhaps *Williams v Roffey*.

Why not just do another search? The answer is the same as the reason given above: to get you into the habit of doing things the right way, which will save a future employer money. If, once you are in practice, you search on one of the commercial databases the supplier will normally charge per search. If you abandon your first search and make another you will be charged twice. If, on the other hand, you do one search and then narrow it you will only pay for one search.

What you need to do is to learn how to search without being too wide in the first place and, if you are, how to narrow your search. For example:

Scenario

> You have been given an essay to do about economic loss in negligence. Although your lecturers will have started this area with the case of *Donoghue v Stevenson*, do not start your search with that or just using 'negligence' as your search term. The database will probably tell you there are too many sources to list. If you start more narrowly, possibly using a combination of 'negligence', 'economic loss' and '*Caparo*' (a more modern case on the area which you will have found from your lecture notes or textbook), this will give you a more manageable search result. Specifying only articles from the last 2 or 3 years – that is, those the textbooks are less likely to cite – is even better.

The specialist law databases have their own factsheets, training materials and tutorial material to teach you to use them. Not surprisingly, they all work slightly differently, so make sure you have the materials handy for when you need to search for something.

What other secondary sources might be useful? One set of sources that is much neglected is papers from the Law Commission. The Law Commission is a body set up by an Act of Parliament to make recommendations for law reform. The Commission either identifies areas for itself or is asked to undertake reform of an area by the Government, and it publishes programmes of projects. It then publishes a Consultation Paper on the area, which explores it in detail, providing a very thorough discussion, masses of reference material, options for reform and discussion of them. These papers are invaluable. For example:

Scenario

> You have been set an assignment on liability for conspiracy to commit a crime. Law Commission Consultation Paper 183 should be on your reading list for this area of law. It was published in 2007, and will give you a thorough and authoritative examination of the topic.

Once the consultation period is complete, the Commission will review what they have done in the light of views submitted and will usually then publish a Report with proposals for reform and frequently a draft Bill. These reports are less use as they refer back to the Consultation Paper rather than repeating it but they do tend to promote a rash of journal articles that are likely to be of use to you. For example:

Scenario

For the same assignment on conspiracy, if you use a slightly earlier Law Commission Report, *Inchoate Liability for Assisting and Encouraging Crime*, Law Commission 300, as your search term it will produce recent articles on the area. Use either the title or 'Law Commission 300', not both.

There is a great deal more material available online and free. The issue to consider again is quality control and the agenda of the person or body publishing it. Even publications from government departments and professional bodies have their own agendas, not all of which are acknowledged. Other organisations may be pushing overt lines or they may not. As a general rule we would recommend that you avoid the use of such materials.

Problems of authority

Are there any problems with using materials even though they are authoritative? Yes, there are. There are very good reasons for this. Court judgments (particularly from the higher courts) and academic publications are about questioning the law and expanding it. Academics debate areas of law from differing perspectives and so will come to different conclusions. This is what being an academic is about. This means that what has been written can be found subsequently to be wrong as a result of legal developments. For example, Lord Denning was an important judge for many years as Master of the Rolls, the head of the Court of Appeal. He said in a series of cases that 'contractual licences now have a force and validity of their own and cannot be breached ...' However, as you will learn, there is no such thing as an irrevocable licence and subsequently orthodoxy was restored and this part of the line of cases overruled. Textbooks and your tutors should tell you when this happens but some do get it wrong.

Also some authors do produce errors – mistakes which we would penalise a student for. One example, based on a real one, is:

In fact the case is currently before the EU Grand Chamber.

The Grand Chamber is a court of the European Court of Human Rights, not the EU! Similarly, in two recent books we have found that the authors wrote:

> The judge said in an obiter that ...

This is wrong. In the expression *obiter dictum*, a thing said by the way, the noun, the naming word, is *dictum*. *Obiter* is an adjective, a word which accompanies a noun, and it can be used as an adverb, a word which accompanies a verb, but in both cases it is a qualifying word, it cannot be used as a noun as these authors did. We will see more about this in Chapter 6 (p. 53).

We said that the important thing about these authoritative sources is that they can be relied on because of the process they go through, which makes them authoritative. Now we are saying they may be wrong – so how do you know what you can rely on? The answer is that if you write something based on an academic opinion which your tutors do not share, you will not be penalised for it as long as the authority you are citing is properly referenced. We will look at this in Chapter 5 (p. 38). If your tutors are not familiar with the author's work, they will be able to check that you have cited it correctly and give you credit for that. As we said earlier, academic debate is about disagreeing and, until a matter is settled by legislation or a judgment, expressing different opinions is what drives the development of the law.

Similarly, something can appear to be settled law for many years and then a new judgment will throw the whole area into confusion again. For example, ever since the case of *Stilk v Myrick* in 1809 it had been the view that an agreement for extra consideration for performance of an existing contractual duty could never be enforced in law. The Court of Appeal in *Williams v Roffey* in 1990 said that this view was not always right and the decision in the earlier case had been for an additional different reason. As a result, nearly 200 years of authority had to be reconsidered to differentiate between those circumstances in which *Stilk v Myrick* was still good authority and those circumstances where the principle applied in *Williams v Roffey* ruled. This shows that even where the law appears to be settled it can still be questioned and brought into debate. What you must do is make your authority for this questioning clear to those who are marking your work.

Demonstrating authority

How do you make sure your authority shows? When you have written a paragraph, read it back to yourself. Where is the authority for what you have said? Is it clear from what you have read back – or is it in your head or the notes you have made preparing for the assignment, or somewhere else? The marker cannot see these other places. Put the authority where your marker can see it, on the page. How you enable your marker to see it will vary depending on the type of assessment you are producing, as we will see later, but they all have one thing in common: it has to be there.

You also need to make sure that you are using your sources in an appropriate way. Do not simply reproduce what they have said without thinking. These are examples that we have seen:

> **Example 1: inaccurate statement**
>
> The Law of Property (Miscellaneous Provisions) Act 1989 has recently introduced a new set of provisions relating to contracts made by deed.

The article which the student used as authority for this was written in 1991 so, to its author, the provision was recent. Over 20 years later that is definitely not the case. So how would you use that article as your authority without that error? One way, if you are paraphrasing the article, would be to say:

> **Improved answer 1**
>
> The Law of Property (Miscellaneous Provisions) Act 1989 introduced a new set of provisions relating to contracts made by deed.

You then reference the article. Alternatively, you could quote the author directly whilst making sure that you recognise that the change is not recent. For example:

> **Improved answer 2**
>
> Smith wrote in her article in 1991 that: 'The Law of Property (Miscellaneous Provisions) Act 1989 introduced a new set of provisions relating to contracts made by deed.'

Either of these is fine. You have not only used your authority but you have used it appropriately so that the marker of your work can tell that you understand what you have said and have provided your authority.

Another example we have seen is:

Example 2: inaccurate statement

It is estimated that, once in force, the Commonhold and Leasehold Reform Act 2002 will enable more than 1.5 million people to own their flats outright.

When this was written, between the Act being passed in 2002 and its coming into force in 2004, it was correct. Now it is not. So how would you use it? Again, you could use one of two ways. Either:

Improved answer 1

It was estimated before the Commonhold and Leasehold Reform Act 2002 came into force that it would enable more than 1.5 million people to own their flats outright. However, this turned out not to be the case.

Once again, reference your source. An alternative would be:

Improved answer 2

As Powell wrote in 2003: 'It is estimated that the Commonhold and Leasehold Reform Act 2002 will enable more than 1.5 million people to own their flats outright.' The Act came into force in 2004 and it has since become apparent that this will not happen.

You have correctly quoted your authority and confirmed to the marker that you understand that the author was writing before the Act came into force.

Another example was:

Example 3: inaccurate statement

In the recent case of *Cassis de Dijon* the court held that ...

So, what is wrong with that? The first thing is that the case was decided in 1979! The student was citing an article from 1980 when the decision was recent. The second thing one might question is: why is a student using an article from 1980 at all? The jurisprudence has developed considerably since then and more recent articles would be more relevant. It was particularly ironic that the 'recent' case was older than the student.

The lesson to learn from these examples is both to make sure that the authority you are citing is as up to date as possible and that you use it critically, not just copying what the author has written but using it appropriately, avoiding the errors we have just seen.

Summary

In this chapter we have:

- looked at sources of authority in law;
- divided them into primary sources (legislation and cases) and secondary sources (textbooks, journal articles and others);
- explained what makes a source authoritative and so safe to use, and what sources you should not use and why;
- shown how to incorporate these sources into your work appropriately and how to avoid some of the common pitfalls.

5 Referencing

By the end of this chapter you should be able to:

▶ understand why referencing is important;
▶ be able to reference primary and secondary sources;
▶ recognise what plagiarism is and be able to avoid it.

● The reasons for referencing

We said we would come to referencing and you have probably understood from the earlier chapters one of the reasons that it is necessary: to provide the source of your authority so that your tutors will know that you have researched your topic and understand how authority works to provide the underpinning needed for an academic piece of work. There is a second reason which you might not have thought of: that is, the avoidance of plagiarism. Plagiarism is passing off someone else's work as your own and is serious in any academic field but particularly so in law.

All academic writing depends on authority and this is especially so in academic law writing. The last thing a tutor wants to read in your work is expressions such as 'I think' or 'I believe'. The tutor is entitled to say 'So what?' because you are not an academic authority. You do draw conclusions but we will show you how to do this with authority. You may think that some of what we tell you is simplistic because you cannot imagine how anyone could get it wrong. However, all the examples we are using are instances where we have had students get it wrong!

● Acts of Parliament

The most compelling form of authority is an Act of Parliament. By virtue of being an Act it is the law and it is very easy to cite. For example, if you are producing an assignment on theft the one thing you almost certainly will need is the definition of theft and this is found in Theft Act 1968 s 1. As a result you will need to say:

Example 1: citing an Act of Parliament

The Theft Act 1968 states that:

> A person is guilty of theft if he dishonestly appropriates property belonging to another with the intention of permanently depriving the other of it;

followed by a reference in a footnote to s 1 such as:

Theft Act 1968 s 1

An alternative would be:

Example 2: citing an Act of Parliament

Theft is defined in Theft Act 1968 s 1 which states that:

> A person is guilty of theft if he dishonestly appropriates property belonging to another with the intention of permanently depriving the other of it;

You might think that this is easy enough, and it is, but students still get it wrong by not sticking to these simple and straightforward models.

If you look at a print copy of the Theft Act 1968 you will see that it has on it a chapter number, in this case Chapter 60. What does this mean? It merely means that this was the sixtieth Act of Parliament to be passed in that session. It used to be important because Acts did not have what is known as the Short Title and so they were referenced by the year of the reign of the king or queen and the chapter number. As all Acts now do have a Short Title, you can find it in the Act itself, in this case in s 36(1) and it reads:

This Act may be cited as the Theft Act 1968.

You have the authority of the Act for citing it this way, so do so. Something else you will also see in the Act is what is called the Long Title. In this instance:

> An Act to revise the law of England and Wales as to theft and similar
> or associated offences, and in connection therewith to make provision
> as to criminal proceedings by one party to a marriage against the
> other, and to make certain amendments extending beyond England
> and Wales in the Post Office Act 1953 and other enactments; and for
> other purposes connected therewith.

It is placed after the Coat of Arms. Just as you do not cite the chapter number, you do not cite this either (although in certain instances it might be useful as a guide to what the intention behind the Act is). Courts have frequently carried out such an exercise in interpreting an Act.

Acts of Parliament are also referred to as statutes or legislation, sometimes as primary legislation. All these terms are correct and you can use them; it is just that 'Act of Parliament' or more frequently 'Act' is simple and the simplest way is often the best.

In addition to Acts of Parliament, there is also what is referred to as secondary legislation. This is just as much the law as primary legislation, provided it has been enacted in accordance with the authority for it, that is, authority contained in an Act of Parliament.

● Secondary legislation

The most important and most voluminous source of secondary legislation is the Statutory Instrument, also referred to as Regulations. These are produced by a government minister and laid before Parliament. Some require Parliamentary votes in both the House of Commons and the House of Lords but most do not; they come into effect a set time after being placed before Parliament unless a resolution is passed stating that they do not. Even those Statutory Instruments requiring a vote are much easier to pass than Acts themselves and so this is an easy way for ministers to get important but detailed material into law. You can see how important these are by the fact that in 2008 Parliament passed 33 Public General Acts. In the same year there were Statutory Instruments numbered up to 3327. This does not mean there were quite that many Statutory Instruments because some numbers end up not being used, but it gives you a good idea of the scale: something around one hundred times as many.

As we have said, since Statutory Instruments are themselves law you cite them as you would an Act, for example that Number 3327 in 2008 as:

> **Example: citing a Statutory Instrument**
>
> The Civil Procedure (Amendment No.3) Rules 2008
>
> However, in this case, either after the name or as a footnote, you would also cite the number and year, so this becomes:
>
> The Civil Procedure (Amendment No.3) Rules 2008 SI 2008/3327

The other source of secondary legislation which you might need to cite is byelaws. These are laws, again passed under the authority of an Act of Parliament, to apply in a particular place. The most common are byelaws of a local authority: the council for an area passes a byelaw to cover the whole of the authority's area or just parts of it, commonly under the authority of the Local Government Act 1982. A fairly common example of the latter are byelaws which prohibit drinking alcohol in certain streets or parks. Many other bodies have authority to pass byelaws too. Some are private companies, but citation of them is generally fairly simple: the local authority or other body and the name of the byelaws, for example:

> **Example: citing byelaws**
>
> The Anytown Earpiercing and Electrolysis Byelaws

In case you are wondering, apart from 'Anytown' replacing the name of the real local authority, these are real byelaws. You will not need to cite such things very often but it is useful to know how.

Cases

Citation of cases is easy in many respects and you will see from what your lecturers give you or from textbooks that the starting point is the names of the two parties. In civil cases that would be, for example:

> **Example 1: citing cases**
>
> *Smith v Jones*

The 'v' should always be said as 'and' – or, less commonly, 'against' – never 'vee' or 'versus'. The order is important. If this is a first instance decision, Smith is the **claimant** and Jones the **defendant**; if it is an appeal then Smith is the one who is appealing, referred to as the **appellant**, and Jones is the **respondent**.

In most criminal cases the citation is:

Example 2: citing cases

R v Smith

The prosecution is undertaken on behalf of the Crown and the 'R' is short for 'Regina' which is Latin for 'the Queen'. When there is a King it is short for 'Rex'. There are some criminal cases prosecuted by other bodies, such as local authorities, where the citation is as it is in civil cases. These are the most common case citations you will use throughout your course.

However, as with anything in law there are complications. You will see cases cited as:

Example 3: citing cases

Re C

This means 'In the matter of C' and the initial is being used instead of a name to preserve the anonymity of 'C'. This is used commonly where the application is about a child or about medical treatment. It used to be that although you wrote '*Re C*', or '*In re. C*', you said 'In the matter of'. This has tended to die away and 'Re C' is now acceptable as both the written and spoken form.

Sometimes both parties' names are omitted for reasons of confidentiality, for example:

Example 4: citing cases

Ms B v An NHS Trust

---

where the judge had issued an order against anyone identifying either the applicant or the hospital trust.

The other complication surrounds the citation of cases where the application is for judicial review: that is, an application to the High Court to test the lawfulness of some action. These are cited as:

Example 5: citing cases

R (von Brandenburg) v East London and the City NHS Trust

The 'R' again here is the Crown since all such cases are nominally taken by the Crown but the applicant is von Brandenburg who is challenging the lawfulness of an action taken by the East London and the City NHS Trust. Older cases for judicial review will be cited as:

Example 6: citing cases

R v Bournewood Community and Mental Health NHS Trust ex parte L

Ex parte means 'from one side', as the applicant first applies to the court for permission to apply and the respondent only comes in subsequently. The reason for this is that applicants for judicial review must first apply for leave to bring the case from a judge before the case itself is heard.

It is vital that you do not confuse these three forms, which we have seen done. If you can demonstrate that you do know the difference between, *R v Smith*, *Re Smith* and *R (Smith)* you will look to be knowledgeable and your tutors will consider that you have learned what law is about.

Once you have cited the case name you need to provide a source. This is simple because all cases have neutral citations: that is, citations which do not depend on any particular set of law reports but on the court which made the decision. For a neutral citation you merely need the name of the case, the year of the decision, the court and the number of the decision for that year, for example:

Example: a neutral citation

Sugar v British Broadcasting Corp. [2009] UKHL 9

This means that the person who has appealed is Sugar, the respondent is the BBC, the decision was issued in 2009 and was a decision of the House of Lords (UKHL is United Kingdom House of Lords), and it was the ninth of that year. A list of neutral citations is included in Appendix 3 (p. 204), at the back of this book. As such decisions tend to be fairly long and you need to point your tutors to the place you are citing from, you would then add the paragraph number:

Sugar v British Broadcasting Corp. [2009] UKHL 9 [23]

Neutral citations are a fairly modern phenomenon. Earlier cases are referenced to sets of printed law reports, the year of the report (not of the judgment), the set of reports with possibly a volume number and a page reference. This would look like:

Example: citing law reports

Smith v Jones [1995] 2 AC 420

This is the Law Reports Appeal Cases, 1995, Volume 2 at page 420. A list of common citations and what they mean can be found in Appendix 3 (p. 204). You will frequently see in textbooks and some other sources that cases are given multiple citations. This is to make it easier for someone to find the case but you should not do it; give one citation, the neutral one if there is one, and no more.

Secondary sources

As we said earlier, academic authority is important and citing and referencing accurately are both vital. The easiest of secondary sources to access is probably the textbook as authority. Using it as we described in Chapter 3, you then need to reference it sufficiently so that your tutors can go directly to what you have used as authority. If you have quoted directly from the textbook and have indicated this by the passage being bracketed by quotation marks or by its being indented (or both), you then insert a footnote (modern word-processing technology does it for you) in the following order: author, *text* (edition, publisher, place, date) page number. This version would give:

Example: citing textbooks

D P Powell, *Choosing Life or Death* (2nd edn, Anypublisher London 2009) 420

One problem here is that there are several citation systems, so find out which your university uses and stick to it. We will look at some standard citation forms later.

Similarly, if instead of quoting directly from the text you have paraphrased the author's words, you would use the same referencing to the book. As a result, your tutor can pick up the book and check that what you have said is accurate and so give you credit for it.

If you are citing a journal article, the referencing is: author, article title, year, journal abbreviated title, page. For example:

Example: citing journal articles

E L Smith, 'The European Court of Justice and the Rule of Reason: A Critical Examination' (2009) ELJ 212

If the journal is referenced by a volume number rather than a year, this would go immediately before the journal title, for example:

E L Smith, 'The European Court of Justice and the Rule of Reason: A Critical Examination' (2009) 45 ELJ 212

Again, your tutor can go straight to the article and check what you have said and give you credit for it. Even if you have sourced your journal article from one on the specialist law databases your university has given you access to, reference the article to its original source and not to the database. In fact, you should almost never cite a database because, apart from some unreported cases they may contain, they do not have original material; they have material which has been published elsewhere and they have collected it in one computer-based form. If you do find it necessary to cite an unreported case from a database and it has no other reference, then you can reference the database but in no other instance.

This brings us to the tricky subject of referencing internet material. Generally, if the material is merely an internet version of a published work, cite the published work as we have done above. For example, if you have accessed a Law Commission Consultation Paper via the Law Commission's website, you can cite it as the published version because that is what you will have accessed. So this would be:

Example: citing a Consultation Paper

Law Commission, 'The Illegality Defence: A Consultative Report', Consultation Paper No. 189, para. 4.3

If the material is only available as an internet source, remember what we said about authority earlier and give the full address, not just the site address, and the date you accessed it. The date is needed as it is easy for those posting internet material to change it and your tutor may encounter a different version. If you have given the date, your tutor can check when the entry was last updated. A typical reference would be:

Example: citing internet material

> <http://www.wjli.ac.uk/2009/issue1.Smith01.htm> accessed 6 May 2009

This brings up another factor relating to referencing. When you access any material for your assignment you must make sure that your notes also contain the reference. It is far too easy to have made notes of something and to come back to it later not remembering that it is from a published source and then to write it as your own. If you note the reference every time you access anything, this is less likely to happen.

Referencing systems

One of the problems with referencing is that there are so many different referencing systems. The Harvard system is probably the most common referencing system in use in universities. However, it is not law specific, so it was developed into a law-specific version at Oxford University and is referred to as OSCOLA, The Oxford Standard for Citation of Legal Authorities. It is available at http://denning.law.ox.ac.uk/published/oscola_2006.pdf. If your law school or university does not specify a reference system, then this is a safe one to use. If you are told to use another referencing system then use the one you are told to, not this one. They all have advantages and disadvantages so it is impossible to say that any one is better than another. Check with your tutors which system you should be using and see if there is a factsheet or guide available to show you how to follow it. Your university library should have these both as paper copies and online.

It is easy to get carried away with referencing but you should not need to give full citations to works every time you use them. If you have referenced something and your next reference is later in the same work, you reference in full the first time and then the second time use the term 'ibid.' and the new page or paragraph number. 'Ibid.' is an abbreviation of 'ibidem', which is Latin for 'the same'. If you have cited the work earlier but not as the previous reference you can cross-reference to the earlier citation and add the new page or paragraph number. In this case, either in the text or the footnote you would need to give some further guidance as to which earlier reference you were pointing to, for example:

> ... as Powell (2009) stated ...

and then the reference:

> Powell (n 21) 54

Although OSCOLA states that other abbreviations of Latin terms should not be used, one you will see frequently is 'op. cit.', which is an abbreviation of '*opere citato*', Latin for 'the work cited'.

We explained earlier why referencing is important in order that your work is of a proper academic standard. Learning how to reference properly is well worth the effort as it is something that will be important throughout your academic career. Tutors are frequently disappointed to find that when they read final-year dissertations, students are still making errors which were corrected in year 1. If you have your university's or law school's referencing guide, keep it visible where you work so that you can check that your referencing is correct. If you have not got a guide, flag the relevant pages of this book (pp. 38–47). Once you get into the habit of referencing correctly you will find it takes no effort; if you do not, it will be a handicap to you throughout your academic career.

Plagiarism

We said earlier that there were two important reasons for referencing properly, one positive, the other negative. The positive one is to show the academic authority for what you are saying and the negative one is to avoid plagiarism. Plagiarism is passing off someone else's work as your own. The word 'plagiarism' comes from the Latin word for a kidnapping, which in turn was based on the Greek word for it. You are kidnapping someone's work! The basic instruction is 'Do not do it!'. What we need now is to show you why and how.

So why is plagiarism wrong? The answer is that it is a form of cheating because you are not acknowledging where you got the material from. If anything is sourced from anywhere, reference it.

How does plagiarism happen? It is not always deliberate. There have been instances where students have not known that they had plagiarised something because they had made notes without noting the source and then imagined it was their own work. The tutor has then identified it and discovered the source. The first the student has known of the plagiarism is when they have been notified of formal proceedings.

The most common ways for plagiarism to happen are that someone has copied from another student, or two students have worked so closely together that they have written the same thing, or someone has copied from a printed source such as a textbook or journal article, or has downloaded or copied material from the internet. It used to be that one student copying from another was the most common form of plagiarism but nowadays it is copying internet sources. The growth of the internet and the availability of search engines and sites such as Wikipedia has made finding material that much easier. However, as we said earlier, these sources are problematic (even if they are properly referenced) as they are not authoritative (see p. 26), so do not use them at all. That way you will have avoided one plagiarism possibility automatically.

One of the most important aspects of plagiarism is that it attracts penalties: if you are found guilty of the offence of plagiarism you will be punished for it. Since universities make their own rules, the nature of the penalties varies (you can check what the penalties are at your university by looking at the relevant regulations). Most universities have a range of penalties. It is fairly common for a first offence relating to an assignment to attract a fail mark, following which the student, subject to otherwise satisfactory performance, will be given an opportunity to do another piece of work to pass the subject. However, for second offences, and first offences relating to major works such as dissertations, it may be the case that the mark will be a fail with no opportunity to make good. That would mean failing the degree! One of the saddest experiences for a tutor is to have watched a student develop over the period of their degree course and then to see them leave the university without a degree because of plagiarism.

You will probably have understood by now that being a law student is different from being a student on other courses. There is a different penalty for plagiarism too. If you wish to go on to qualify as a solicitor or barrister, your university will be asked by the Solicitors Regulation Authority or Bar Standards Board to confirm that you have a qualifying law degree. If you have been found guilty of an offence of plagiarism, this may disqualify you; your university has to report such findings with the confirmation of your degree. Although the disqualification is not automatic, obviously the professional bodies have to observe due process, and the student will have to go through a formal procedure. This takes time, so it can mean that entry onto a professional course can be delayed for a year. Commonly it means that the student is barred from entry and so can never qualify. If you are ever tempted to plagiarise, for example because you have left the completion of an assignment until the last minute and think that you will not complete it in time, remember what it might cost. That way you will not do it.

Even if plagiarism does not disqualify you, the finding will always appear on your assessment results and in any reference your university provides so that it will be clear to any future employer that you have cheated on your degree course. It is not a quality that many employers are looking for.

As a result, avoiding plagiarism is important and it is easy to do as long as you follow the referencing instructions you have been given. You need to remember that putting a source in your bibliography will never be enough; the reference must be in the body of the work where the material appears. Here are a few examples of what might – and might not – be plagiarism.

> A paragraph copied verbatim from a source without any acknowledgement. *Plagiarism?*

This obviously is plagiarism and is fairly easy to identify. What many students do not appear to appreciate is that tutors when marking assignments can identify style changes very easily and if one part of the assignment reads differently it raises the possibility of plagiarism.

> A paragraph copied from a source making a few small changes to the wording and listing the source in the bibliography. *Plagiarism?*

This is also plagiarism because minor amendments to the wording do not mean that it is not copied. It is arguable that this is worse than the first example: the student has recognised what they are doing and has tried to hide it. Again, this is easy for the tutor to identify.

> A paragraph copied from a source but omitting one or more sentences and putting the others in a different order. The material is not in quotation marks but there is a reference such as (Powell 2009) and there is a full reference in the bibliography. *Plagiarism?*

This is where opinions start to vary but we consider this is still plagiarism as the student has used complete sentences from the original without identifying them as quotations.

> A paragraph composed by taking short phrases from a number of sources with words added by the student. The source phrases are individually acknowledged in the text and there are full bibliographic references. *Plagiarism?*

The dividing line between 'plagiarism' and 'not plagiarism' is probably here. The paragraph will be plagiarised if the source material is the majority of the paragraph. On the other hand, if the student's own material comprises the major part of the paragraph there is unlikely to be an offence. The only difficulty here is that some plagiarism detection software would identify the paragraph as plagiarised even if it is not. We will come back to that later (see p. 51).

> A paragraph paraphrased with substantial changes in language and organisation, detail and examples. The source phrases are individually acknowledged in the text and there are full bibliographic references. *Plagiarism?*

This is not plagiarism; this is what you are expected to do in those parts of your assignment, the majority of it, in which you are not quoting a source directly.

> A paragraph is placed in block format with the source cited in the text and the bibliography. *Plagiarism?*

Obviously this is not plagiarism; it is what we have told you to do earlier in the chapter if you are quoting a source directly. All you need to be careful of with such a format is ensuring that the whole assignment is not just a collection of quotes with little coherence. This will be examined in more detail later (see p. 55).

One thing that constantly amazes lecturers is how naïve some students are about their lecturers' ability to identify plagiarism. As was said earlier, the writing style of most students is not generally as good as that of most academic authors. If the style in an assignment changes suddenly to a much more polished one it is likely that there is plagiarism. It is then merely a case of tracking down the source.

If a student has copied something from a book or article, it is likely to be a book or article which your tutor has read. This appears to come as a surprise to some students, who seem not to appreciate that academics read academic work. It might take effort to find which source has been copied from but it is frequently the case that the piece copied is individual to a particular author and so the source can be recalled quickly. This has happened to us frequently.

If one student has copied the work of another student, the tutor will mark the first piece they come across and when marking the second piece be struck by the impression that they have read it before. It is then fairly easy to go back through the marked pile to identify the other piece. Obviously, the tutor cannot identify which student did the copying but both will be subject to plagiarism proceedings and both may be considered guilty, either because they have copied from each other or because one allowed the other to copy their work.

As we said earlier, the majority of instances of plagiarism are now a result of internet sources. If the source is a good one, what was said earlier about writing style applies here equally. Once the possibility of plagiarism has been raised it is fairly easy to track the material down. Students frequently appear to be surprised that tutors can identify the material and the source. It is important to remember that if you can find something, your tutor can probably find it the same way.

When faced with the possibility of plagiarism, the tutor has a number of tools available to identify the source material. As noted previously, books and journal articles are likely to be familiar. Even if the journal article is not recognised immediately, it is easy enough to identify since virtually all journal articles are available on the specialist law databases. All the tutor has to do is to search the databases with the suspect material and the source will be identified. The database even highlights the relevant words.

A variety of plagiarism detection software is also available. Most universities now subscribe to one of these packages and tutors can run assignments through them. This is one of the reasons that universities are increasingly turning to electronic assignment submission, frequently through **VLE**s (Virtual Learning Environments), as it enables the tutor to put the whole assignment through the software. It is also the case that universities are making the software available to students so that they can check their work in advance. However, this software needs to be treated with caution. It is useful in relation to the sources it has at its disposal. The problem is that much of the material likely to be used is subject to a publisher's copyright and so may not be available to the package. There is also another problem which applies to all academic disciplines but to law more than most. A law student is expected to use certain expressions because they encapsulate the legal concepts under discussion. Unfortunately, the software will identify these as being plagiarised when they are not. It is not uncommon when using one of these packages to be informed that the work in question is 50 per cent plagiarised when, in fact, all that is identified is the use of the appropriate legal concepts.

Ultimately, for the student, the avoidance of plagiarism is about taking care: ensuring that material in an assignment is appropriately identified and referenced. Follow these simple rules and you need never be worried about falling foul of a plagiarism finding.

Summary

In this chapter we have:

- identified two reasons for referencing being a priority: academic authority and the avoidance of plagiarism;
- looked at forms of referencing for both primary and secondary sources;
- examined the causes and effects of plagiarism and outlined methods for its avoidance.

6 A Sophisticated Approach

By the end of this chapter you should be able to:

▶ understand what a sophisticated approach to writing for law is;
▶ be able to use academic sources correctly;
▶ avoid telling stories in assessments;
▶ appreciate the importance of grammar in assessments.

What is it?

What is a sophisticated approach to writing law assignments? One answer is: the approach which will achieve the top marks, and you do that, as we said earlier, by fulfilling the **learning outcomes** and **marking criteria**. We will look at these in respect of the various types of assessment you are likely to undertake in the later parts of this book but there are some general rules that need to be explored first.

The first of these is that if you are asked to perform a task, perform that task and not a different one. You might think that is obvious but it is not always so. For example, you might be set a question such as this:

Sample question 1

The separation of powers is a fundamental part of the constitution of the United Kingdom. Discuss.

How are you going to approach this question? It is very common for students to start an assignment with very general statements on the area. The question is, what do such statements do to answer the question? If the answer is 'nothing', then they should not be there. An example might be:

Sample answer 1

In this assignment I am going to look at the separation of powers, I am going to examine whether it is a fundamental part of the constitution and I am going to discuss this.

It is hoped that you are going to do these things as this is what you have been asked to do by the question; so do not say you are going to do it.

Introductions

As far as introductions to assignments are concerned there are two approaches, either of which is fine. The first one is: do not do an introduction; go straight into the task. If your tutors had wanted you to do something more general they would have set a different assignment. So if your assignment is the one above, for example, the best way to start is to define what the question means.

Sample answer 2

The separation of powers means that the three elements of government, the legislature, the executive and the judiciary, are independent of each other.

You can then go on to examine the extent to which the constitution fulfils this definition. This approach has the advantage that you are not wasting some of your word limit on material which will not get you any marks; you have started with what the question means and can continue from there.

There is another approach that works if it is done well. This is to start an assignment with a very brief introduction to the subject before tackling the question itself. However, it has the disadvantage that if it is not done well, the assignment can look as though it is starting very badly. If that happens, the tutor marking it will carry that impression with them through their reading of the work, which may result in your assignment not receiving the mark it deserves because of the negative impression you produced at the start. If you take this approach you need to ensure that this introduction is only a few sentences long: a brief paragraph to set the scene generally. For the same assignment this might be:

Sample answer 3

For states with a written constitution it is fairly easy to determine if there is a separation of powers. What the constitution says about the elements of government, along with an examination of the independence of any particular element from the others in practice, can be examined. In the United Kingdom the absence of a written constitution means that the first part of this task has to be an examination of how each element comes into being and by what authority. It is only then that the main task can be tackled.

This is short, 92 words, gives some measure of the task being undertaken and leads the marker into the main body of the work.

The hazard in the second approach is that the introduction can grow to such an extent that it takes over the assignment. If your tutors have set a problem question they do not want an essay for an answer. If they have set the assignment we have given above, they do not want an essay on the unwritten constitution. Yet these are things that students do on occasions and it results in them either failing or earning a poor mark, not because they do not know enough but because they have not done what they were asked to do.

The other common failing at the beginning of assignments is to explain what you are going to do and how you are going to do it. This has two disadvantages. One is that you are using some of your word limit on unnecessary material, which means that you will have to sacrifice other material to accommodate it. The other is that if your assignment does what it should do, what you are doing and how will be obvious; if it does not do what it should do, do not advertise the fact.

Combining sources

The next element of a sophisticated approach is to use a variety of sources. Chapter 4 explained about sources and how to use them individually. This chapter is about putting them together. If the marker sees a series of footnotes all referring to the same judgment, book or article, they will know that what you are doing is listing the views of one judge or writer. It also means that the work is in danger of becoming more about 'what' than 'why', which was discussed in Chapter 3 (p. 13). If you have a variety of sources you need to use them constructively. That means, in general, that you state one view, giving the authority for it, and then another so that you can compare and contrast what the writers are saying. For example, looking at liability for homicide by omission you might say:

Sample answer showing the views of two judges

In *Airedale NHS Trust v Bland* the judges in the House of Lords agreed that it would be lawful for doctors to cease the treatment of Tony Bland with the result that he would die. However, the route by which they reached this conclusion differed. Lord Goff considered that the solution lay in the proposition that the right of self-determination should not be lost by virtue of incompetence. This is approaching, but not quite reaching, a substitute decision test: that is, making the decision the judge believes the patient would have made if he had been capable. Lord Browne-Wilkinson, on the other hand, said that the duty to provide treatment to the incompetent patient ended when the treatment ceased to be of benefit to the patient. Moreover, he said that at that point to continue treatment would be unlawful.

Your sources here are two speeches in the same case. By contrasting these points you have produced a much more powerful argument than you would have done by listing all the elements of one and then going on to do the same for the other. This approach is much more immediate: you can examine one aspect of the decision, before going on to others in the same way.

Similarly, if you are using the views of two authors you can compare and contrast individual points successively to a much better effect than if you just listed what each said. On the same topic you might say:

Sample answer showing the views of two authors

Smith (2009) supports the reasoning of the House of Lords decision in *Airedale NHS Trust v Bland* that there is a dividing line between the lawful withdrawal of medical treatment resulting in death and the unlawful giving of treatment resulting in death. The first is an omission, which is lawful if there is no duty, whereas the second is a deliberate act. However, Powell (2007) disagrees, stating that the dichotomy is false. He considers that each is an act because the treatment is being undertaken. It requires something to be done for that treatment to cease.

Again, you have taken one element of each writer's argument and contrasted them and, as a result, constructed a much more powerful paragraph than you would do by treating each in isolation.

Telling stories

What else have you noticed from these examples? We are not telling stories. Although case facts are often interesting in themselves, they are rarely needed in assignments. When your tutors give you the facts of cases in your lectures they are using them to illustrate how a particular decision was arrived at and to help you to see how the law developed. This is not what you are doing in assignments.

Instead, you are writing an assignment to demonstrate that you have understood how the law works in that area and, in some assignments, that you can apply it to a new set of facts. If you decide to go into the legal professions this is good practice for you as the cases you come across will not be identical to the ones you have studied. If you become a solicitor or barrister you are rarely, if ever, going to need to write an essay but it is good practice for you if you wish to become an academic. University lecturers are expected to write for publication as an essential element of the job. In neither of these situations will you be expected to recite the facts of the cases you are citing, so do not do it in your assignments or exams.

This is an element of the discipline of law which students appear to find very hard. It seems not to matter how many times or how forcefully it is explained that lecturers do not want stories; students tell them anyway. It is arguable that telling stories is easier than answering the question. After all, all you need to do is copy from your lecture notes or textbook. In an examination it is even better because you do not have to think. You can just learn your lecture notes and rewrite them. However, telling stories has two main disadvantages and one further related one.

The first and most obvious disadvantage is that telling stories does not answer the question you have been asked. Your tutors have not asked you to write out the facts of *Airedale NHS Trust v Bland*, for example. You can see from the example that is used above citing this case, how limited are the facts that you need. You do not need any more. This is particularly important in examinations but is equally true of essays, problem questions and other types of assignment. Lecturers lose count of the times they have said to students that what is important is answering the question and that case facts do not do it. Then when the exam papers arrive they are filled with case facts, not answers to the question. As a result these papers receive poor marks and this book is about you earning good ones.

The second main disadvantage is about space. Word limits have been mentioned already, and here is why. What you may have noticed about law assignments, and if you have not it is something you will come to learn, is that they frequently have much lower word limits than assignments in comparable disciplines. This is deliberate. It is very easy to ramble on for several thousand words and eventually reach your destination. In law you need to arrive there briefly and succinctly. To give you practice at doing that, your assignments will be set with tight word limits and your examinations will have time limits. If you use the words or the time telling stories you will not use them to answer the question you have been set. Do not think that it does not matter, that you can breach the word limit on your assignment or write faster in your exam. If you breach the word limit you will be penalised.

What the penalty will be varies between institutions. Some rule that tutors stop reading the assignment when the word limit is reached. This means that your conclusion and possibly more will not be read and will receive no marks. Other institutions allow the whole to be marked but the mark is then reduced by the amount the assignment is over the word limit. That would mean that if your assignment is 10 per cent over the word limit you would lose a whole grade. In examinations a shorter, more considered answer is better than a long rambling one. Spending some of your examination time thinking and planning answers, rather than just writing furiously for the whole duration, yields better marks. We will look at this in more detail later (p. 167).

It was said that there is a further, related disadvantage in addition to the two main ones, and it may surprise you. Students frequently write case facts wrongly. This may seem odd; how can they be wrong? It is remarkably easy. If you are filling your head with case facts it is easy to mix them up or just remember them wrongly. It is also the case, unfortunately, that on occasion textbooks and journal articles have case facts which are wrong. These should be picked up during the writing and editing process but sometimes it does not happen. There are cases that are notorious for this, the House of Lords' decision in *Gillick v West Norfolk and Wisbech Area Health Authority* being one of them. There have been some amazing distortions of this case with facts bearing no relation to the real ones. So remember: if you do not tell stories you cannot be wrong.

Good English

The next element of a sophisticated approach is English. You may have been told when you were at school or college that the English did not matter as long as you communicated your ideas. This is not true in law, particularly at university level. There are many reasons for this. One is that in marking schemes there is usually a presentation element and this demands correct English. The second is that your tutors will expect correct English and so will penalise any work in which the English is poor. The third is that if your tutors are reading a piece of work in which the English is poor, it will predispose them to not give sufficient credit for the content of the assignment. Obviously, these are all elements of the same thing: poor English is going to cost you marks. The study of law is all about the use of English. You will learn fairly early in your course that the interpretation of an Act of Parliament, and so the outcome of a case, frequently hinges on the meaning of one word.

If, from when you start your course (or preferably before), you ensure that your written English is good it will pay off throughout your course, result in a better degree and help you to go on to the next stage of your life. The opposite is also true. If your written English is poor and you do nothing about it, it will result in the marks throughout your course being poor, producing a poor degree and hampering your chances thereafter. If you think that you have a problem with your written English or if your tutors identify one, do something about it immediately. Do not think it does not matter or that you will find the time later. It *does* matter and you will probably not find the time later. Many university law schools diagnose problems in written English in a student's first week at university. They then advise them of the help available and urge them to use it. Some have a dedicated unit in their library or student services department which does this, and it works wonders with students who go. It cannot do anything for those who do not go. It is likely your university has something similar. Ask about it. There are also some very good online packages available. Your university should have one: check on your library homepage. Or you can find open access packages at other university sites or national sites such as the UK Centre for Legal Education, www.ukcle.ac.uk.

Using your computer's facilities

You also have some help at your fingertips, literally – your computer. Almost all coursework you do will have a requirement that it is word-processed and, obviously, your word-processing software has spell check and grammar packages which will automatically alert you to any problems. However, there are important reservations about these packages. The first thing you need to ensure is that your computer is set to the right language! This might seem odd but when computers are loaded with their software they are frequently set on other languages. Tutors often receive assignments, and also communications from other academics who should know better, set on English (US) or English (Aust.). They know this because it is now quite common for students to submit assignments electronically either via their **VLE** or directly to the tutor. There is nothing wrong with either of these if you are submitting your assignment in the United States or Australia but if you are submitting in the United Kingdom, the setting should be English (UK). It is easy to change, just look it up in your Help package if you do not know how to do it.

The first important reservation is that sophisticated legal writing often offends some grammar rules. This is particularly so in respect of sentence structure, which can appear very complicated. This is necessary in some instances where the ideas are complex; however, a computer grammar check would mark it as wrong. This type of structure has been avoided as much as possible in this book; in most instances the simple way of saying something is best, but on occasions it is unavoidable. If your word-processing package marks something as bad grammar, look at it carefully; if you have learned what good grammar is, you can break some of the rules when necessary.

A grammar package will also not pick up faults that are to do with the conventions of legal writing. For example, the word 'I' should never appear in an academic legal text yet a grammar check would not show this as wrong.

The importance of proofreading

The second important reservation is that a spell check will try to match what you have written to a word in its dictionary. Do not rely on it being the correct one. Here are some examples we have seen:

- The case of *Lampleigh v Brathwait* in a contract assignment came out as *Lamplight v Bathwater*.
- One student's assignment referred throughout to the pineapples (rather than principles) of the Data Protection Act.
- One criminal law assignment rendered 'malice aforethought' as 'malicious afterthought'.
- In a dissertation the student was attempting to use the analogy that a person 'was caught in the tentacles of the Child Support Agency' but it did not quite come out like that!

The answer to this problem is to ensure that you read your work carefully when it is finished. It is easy to be so excited or relieved that you have finished an assignment that you forget to proofread it. It is also helpful, if it is possible, for someone else to proofread it but make sure you do not ask someone who is doing the same assignment because that produces a risk of plagiarism.

Capital letters

Another thing which your spell check facility will not pick up is incorrect use of capital letters. The rule here is fairly straightforward. If you are referring to a specific person or thing, use capital letters; if you are referring to them generically, use lower case. This is what we mean:

Use of capital letters

- Use Parliament if referring to the parliaments of the United Kingdom or Scotland.
- Say the Prime Minister but prime ministers.
- Write Community law and English law but national law.
- When you are referring to legislation it must always be in capitals, so the Law of Property Act and the Act. You should never write 'the act' unless you are meaning what someone has done.

This last one is a problem as newspaper style guides mostly say use lower case; that is fine for a newspaper but not for an assignment. There was an earlier reference to the problems of using newspapers as sources (p. 27), and this is another one. If in doubt about using capitals, the rule given holds generally but have a look at a textbook which contains the material and follow what they do; it should be correct.

Apostrophes

There are also difficulties over apostrophes – these are widely used wrongly. The most common fault is the use of an apostrophe when there ought not to be one. This is usually referred to as 'the grocer's apostrophe' as it is commonly found in food shops and consists of a plural with an apostrophe inserted before the letter 's'.

- In shops the produce is labelled as *potato's* instead of *potatoes*, as *strawberry's* for *strawberries* and *banana's* for *bananas*.
- A local window fitter has on his van *Window's* and a café next to the university offers *Student Meal Deals* (correct) on one side of its sign and *Student Meal Deal's* (incorrect) on the other.

Apostrophes have two uses. The first is to show ownership or belonging. So:

Apostrophes to show ownership or belonging
A man's nose means *the nose of the man*.
The court's judgment means *the judgment of the court*.
The courts' judgments means *the judgments of the courts*.
The Act's short title means *the short title of the Act*.

Using apostrophes in this way in your work is perfectly acceptable but make sure you are using them correctly by testing what you have written: say it in the 'of the' construction and see if it makes sense. If it does you are using the apostrophe correctly. There is one important qualification to this rule:

> **Remember ...**
> Belonging to it is *its* not *it's* or *its'*.

It is also important that apostrophes are not used with plurals of initials but this is very common in books, articles, newspapers and just about anywhere else. Again, a little care can avoid the problem:

> **No apostrophes with initials**
> Members of Parliament are *MPs* not *MP's*.
> Computers and recording devices use *CDs* not *CD's*.
> The decade was the *1990s* not the *1990's*.

The other use of the apostrophe is to denote letters that have been missed out so that the word is contracted. This should only be done when quoting what someone has said, that is, reported speech. As this is rarely done in law assignments, the best rule here is do not use apostrophes in these cases but write the words out in full. Some examples are:

> **Apostrophes to show contraction**
> *He wouldn't* is a contraction of *he would not*.
> *She should've* is a contraction of *she should have*, which has even been seen written as *she should of*!

The reason for saying do not use the apostrophe in this form is twofold. The most important one is that academic writing should be formal and contractions are informal. They are a way of simplifying speech and are the opposite of a sophisticated approach. Again, unfortunately newspapers commonly write this way; you should not. The second reason is a practical one: if for every time you use an apostrophe you use the "of the" test, it will not work with this construction. It means something different so would need a different test. If you avoid contractions completely, there is no problem as you do not need another test.

Slang

Similarly, do not use slang or colloquial expressions. The reason for this is the same as the others: slang and colloquialisms are elements found in everyday speech but they are informal. What you are meant to be writing is a formal piece of work. Slang and colloquial expressions are the opposite. As a result, if you use them you will be adopting the informal tone, which directly contradicts the sophisticated approach being advocated here. If you are not sure if a word is slang or colloquial, look it up in a dictionary. After the word it will show (*sl.*) if the word is slang and (*colloq.*) if it is colloquial.

Use a dictionary

Having a decent dictionary is very worthwhile. You might think that you do not need one, as your spell check and grammar packages will tell you when something you have written is wrong. Subject to the reservations we have already told you about, this is true – but they will not always tell you why something is wrong. You do not need to spend much to get a decent dictionary; a single-volume concise dictionary is enough. What is important about it is that it shows what parts of speech the words are – that is, what is a noun, a verb, an adjective or an adverb. It is sometimes difficult to remember which of two very similar words you should use in which part of speech and a dictionary will tell you. For example:

> *Licence* is a noun, as in *driving licence*; note the change in spelling for the verb *to license* in *the local authority licenses street traders*.

Similarly, if you use a word wrongly it is likely that your software will mark it as wrong but not necessarily tell you why it is wrong and what to do to put it right. For example:

> If you write *the data is confusing*, your package should show that this is wrong, though not all do. So why is it wrong? The word *data* is plural; the singular is *datum*, but some authorities now accept *data* as singular. So you should write *the data are confusing*.

These problems are particularly acute with words that have come from other languages because quite often how they are used in English comes from that language too. The example above is from Latin, the one below from Greek.

> If you write *the criteria for a particular appointment is that the candidate has a law degree*, this is wrong. Why? Because the word *criteria* is plural; the singular is *criterion*. So what you should have written is *the criterion is that the candidate has a law degree* or *one of the criteria is that the candidate has a law degree*.

Probably the most frequent error in student assignments as far as the English is concerned is sentences which lack an active verb. For example:

> **No active verb**
> The defendant was found not guilty. The reason being that no crime
> had been committed.

The first sentence is fine but the second is not. The word 'being' is not an active verb; it is a participle and in general verbs ending with 'ing' are participles which need another verb to make them active. Here the noun 'reason' has no active verb to support it. There are two ways of solving this problem. The first is to replace the participle with an active verb:

> **No active verb: solution 1**
> The defendant was found not guilty. The reason was that no crime
> had been committed.

The other is to change the structure so that the original second sentence becomes a phrase which is part of the first sentence:

> **No active verb: solution 2**
> The defendant was found not guilty: the reason being that no crime
> had been committed.

Of course, the most important thing about having a dictionary is using it. Do not put it on your bookshelf and leave it there; put it on the table or desk you work at so that when you need to look something up you do not have to move to reach it.

Some words are particularly problematic in law assignments because they are used wrongly more frequently than they are used correctly. Probably the most common of these is the word 'literally'. You may recall that we used it earlier when we said that the answer to some of the problems with English was literally at your fingertips, your computer. This is fine because when you are producing your assignment you are typing it on your computer keyboard so the keyboard, and by extension the computer, is literally at your fingertips. What the word 'literally' is often used for is to emphasise the strength of something, as in:

> The footballer worked so hard that he literally died for his team.

He may have died for his team figuratively but he did not do so literally, as he is not dead. The easiest solution to this problem is probably not to use the word 'literally' at all. If you do use it, make sure you use it in its proper sense.

Another thing that neither your spell check nor dictionary will tell you is when there are conventions in legal writing that something is done in a particular way. The most important as far as law assignments are concerned is the word 'judgment'. Although in English it is correct to spell this as either 'judgment' or 'judgement', it is always spelled as *judgment* in law writing, no 'e' in the middle. Similarly, when typing case names you must always use a lower-case 'v', never 'V'. This can be difficult as some spell checks automatically convert single letters to capitals. The solution to this is again proof-reading: make sure you read your assignment immediately before printing it or submitting it electronically, to ensure none of these problems have crept in.

Presentation

The final, general element of the sophisticated approach is the presentation of your assignment. If your university has provided you with presentation guidelines, follow them. If you have not been provided with any, the following are general guidelines which should help you to produce an assignment your tutors will want to read. The first thing to consider is why you need to present your work in a particular way. The answer, as with so many things in this book, is that better presentation equals better marks and poor presentation equals worse ones.

Firstly, make sure that you have a front sheet which specifies the course and year, the module the assignment is for, the module leader or tutor for whom the assignment is written, the assignment title and your name or, if you submit anonymously, your identifying number (see Figure 6.1). This, and any other information you have been asked to include on the front sheet, is all that should be on it. You may think that if you hand in assignments with an additional institution cover sheet that contains much if not all this information, you do not need to do it yourself. This is not true. An institution front sheet normally serves the function of providing you with a receipt for your assignment and the university with a record that you have submitted it. These are often detached from the assignment before marking so that if there is no other identification on the assignment it then requires detective work to find out who it belongs to.

Most importantly, make sure that what you put on the front sheet is accurate. If you write the title of the assignment wrong, it creates the wrong impression from the start. You are trying to create a good impression. It is also useful if you spell the tutor's name correctly. Tutors have seen variations, some of which are amusing – but if you do not know who your module

---

Someplace University

Faculty of Law

LL.B.

Year 1

The Law of Contract

LAW1006

Module Leader: Emma Teare

The requirement for consideration in the English law of contract is an unnecessary

complication which is being systematically eroded by the courts.

Discuss.

Annabelle Student

D0975638

Figure 6.1   Sample front page

leader or tutor is, it suggests that you probably do not know much of the subject either.

Do not, under any circumstances, put a graphic on your front cover. The ones tutors see most commonly are the Scales of Justice and the judge with a wig and a gavel (a small wooden hammer). Judges increasingly do not wear wigs, particularly in civil cases, and English courts do not use gavels. Such an image is likely to make the marker think that the student should have spent more time on the assignment and less time on the cover and, as you are trying to do the opposite, do not do it.

The assignment proper should start on the next page. Use a clear typeface and line spacing. If you have been instructed to use a particular typeface and line spacing, then do so. If not, typefaces such as Arial are generally preferred to the more decorated ones like Times New Roman or Courier because they provide a cleaner look and are easier to read. The print size should never be less than 12 point. Producing an assignment in 10-point print, or even more extreme 8 point, is likely to give the marker eye strain and a headache. Neither of these is going to leave them wanting to award a high mark. Line spacing should be either 1.5 lines or 2 lines; you can set this on the Page Setup or Paragraph setting on your word-processing package.

Unless you have been asked to write a report, which is unlikely in law although common in a number of other subjects, do not use headings and subheadings. They are used in this book to enable you to dip in and out of it to find what you want quickly but this is not necessary, and is positively undesirable, in most types of assignment.

In the body of your assignment separate each point into individual para-graphs and each paragraph into sentences containing the individual compo-nents of that point. There is little that is more discouraging to a marker than to see a whole side of paper filled with print with no indication as to where one point ends and another begins.

Case names should be in *italics*. The convention when assignments were handwritten was that case names were underlined and that is still the case for handwritten examination papers, although some students prefer to use different coloured pens. What is important is that the case name stands out from the rest of the material.

Footnotes should generally be used only for referencing unless you have been instructed otherwise. So, for example, if you cite a case, put the case name in the body of your work but the citation as a footnote. Similarly with references to textbooks or articles: reference the author in the main body of the text, 'Smith (2009)', for example, and give the full reference in a footnote the first time the work is cited and thereafter, *ibid*. or '(Smith n XX)'. With each reference do not forget to add the page and/or paragraph number. With word-processing software this is easy, as you will have an Insert Footnote button in your package which numbers footnotes automatically, and renum-bers them if you insert an extra one later. Do not carry on the argument of your assignment in footnotes. This is sometimes done in textbooks and journal articles to point the reader in the direction of further reading or a point of contrasting argument, and it might be possible for you to develop this ability. However, the marker should be able to read through the assign-ment without referring to the footnotes and understand what you are saying. Some students think that they can use footnotes to carry on the argument and so get round word limits. Your tutors will know that and if you do continue the assignment in your footnotes they will count those as part of your word limit.

At the end of your work, and on a separate page, you should do a bibliography. This should list your sources separately and in alphabetical order by textbooks, journal articles and websites. Some institutions ask for primary sources, Acts and cases, to be entered as well. These should be as a separate list of sources used. Do not be tempted to pad your bibliography out with materials you have not used. Every item in your bibliography should have appeared in a footnote. If an item appears in your bibliography but has not featured in the assignment your tutor is entitled to ask why not. If it would not have contributed anything to the assignment, it has no place in the bibliography; if it would have, it should have been used. It is fairly common to see impressive bibliographies at the end of unimpressive pieces of work. If the student had used the sources they claim, the work would have been better. Make sure yours is. How each type of source is referenced is covered in Chapter 5.

Do not include search engines or databases in your bibliography; they are not sources. What you include are what they produced, journal articles and web pages, and it is these that should be referenced. There is little more dispiriting to a marker than to see these in the bibliography – effectively the student is advertising that they do not know what they are doing.

Although the content of your assignment is the most important element, an assignment which looks good is more impressive, easier to mark and likely to produce a better result than one which does not. Make yours stand out.

Summary

This chapter has looked at:

- what constitutes a sophisticated approach to writing law assignments;
- how to answer the question the tutor has set using a wide range of authority, both primary sources and secondary ones;
- the need to avoid reciting case facts;
- how to use the English language correctly, particularly in terms of the grammar employed;
- the uses and limitations of grammar and spell checks in computer packages;
- the importance of presentation and how to get it right.

Part 2

Essays

7 Where Do I Start?

By the end of this chapter you should be able to:

► use assignment instructions to produce your essay;
► identify the key elements of the essay question;
► decode essay questions.

● Getting your essay title

You have been given an essay title and have been instructed to submit the essay by a specific date. What do you do? Apart from putting it off, which we will come back to, a common reaction is panic. What am I supposed to do? Although you may have been used to writing essays for school or college you have probably been given considerable guidance on them and you may have been able to submit drafts for correction before submitting the final piece of work. On a university law course this is unlikely to happen – the first submission is the real one. You will also have been given a word limit, typically 1500 to 2500 words, and have been told it must not be exceeded. This frequently produces one of two responses:

- ● How do I find that much to say about what appears to be a very simple question?

  or
- ● How do I fit it all in?

The answer to the first one is that although the question may be simple, you can be fairly certain that the answer is unlikely to be. The answer to the second is that you need to decide what is relevant to your answer and what is superfluous. If you have read the first part of this book and remembered its lessons then you are a good deal of the way there. This part will help you to finish your journey.

● Learning outcomes

The first thing you need to look at is: what is the purpose of an essay? To help you with this you may have been provided with a set of **learning outcomes** telling you what your tutors are looking for in the assignment. These were covered in Chapter 2 (p. 10). If you have been provided with these – with the assignment, in your course handbook or with your general course documentation – then use them. If you have not been given any then use the model ones we have provided in Appendix 2, for the particular level appropriate to the essay. What you will notice about these learning outcomes is that they are requiring you to do not just one thing but several. As a result you will need to address the question across this range of outcomes.

The first and most basic outcome concerns 'knowledge and understanding'. Can you demonstrate that you know what the area of law is about? Whilst this is the most basic of the learning outcomes, it is probably the most important since without it you will not be able to move on to the rest. The starting point for this is the materials you have from your lectures and seminars. Did you understand the lectures and did you use the seminars to raise any points you were unsure of? If you did, your grounding in the area should be secure.

The second level of learning outcomes is 'cognitive and intellectual skills'. This is the ability not just to repeat what you have been told but to analyse and apply the current law and, increasingly as you go through your programme of study, to identify problems and propose solutions. The essay question is not asking you to reproduce your notes or part of a textbook, nor is it asking you to give the detailed facts of cases or tell stories (see Chapter 6, p. 56).

The third level is that of practical and professional skills. Can you research the question without being told where to look and can you cite your sources accurately? This has already been covered but if at any point you are unsure, go back to the relevant chapter and check; it is in Chapter 4 from p. 29. This is probably all you will be asked at Level 1 but as you progress you will be expected to be critical and to question increasingly what the authorities are telling you.

The fourth level of learning outcomes relates to general or transferable skills. Can you use legal terminology accurately and can you write effectively to transmit your ideas? The basis for this has already been covered but, again, if you are unsure, go back and check in Chapter 6 (pp. 53–68).

Using learning outcomes

You have the tools for doing the job; now you can use them. What does your assignment title mean? Here are some fairly typical Level 1 assignment essay titles:

Sample question 1

Legal method

'The rules as to precedent reflect the practice of the courts and have to be applied bearing in mind that their objective is to assist in the administration of justice. They are of considerable importance because of their role in achieving the appropriate degree of certainty as to the law. This is an important requirement of any system of justice. The principles should not, however, be regarded as so rigid that they cannot develop in order to meet contemporary needs.'

R. v Simpson [2003] EWCA Crim 1499 [27], [2004] Q.B. 118 (Lord Woolf CJ)

Discuss the above quotation with regard to certainty and flexibility within the doctrine of judicial precedent.

So how do you decode something like this – what is it asking you? The most important element of the question is the instruction so you will need to consider this before considering the quotation. You will note that with most essay questions the instruction will include the word 'discuss'. At this level you might get more guidance on exactly what to discuss, as in this instance pointing you to the opposing considerations of certainty and flexibility, but later it is likely that the instruction will be merely 'discuss' or 'discuss critically'. The key to this question is the opposition of the two concepts of certainty and flexibility, so in discussing judicial precedent you need to state what the rules are, what the exceptions to those rules are, and how far these rules and exceptions provide a balance between certainty and flexibility. You can see here the learning outcomes of 'knowledge and understanding' and 'cognitive and intellectual skills' combining to give an answer. Generally, knowledge and understanding are addressed by stating the rules and exceptions, and cognitive and intellectual skills are demonstrated in stating the balance between certainty and flexibility.

Sample question 2

Constitutional law

The separation of powers is a fundamental part of the constitution of the United Kingdom.

Discuss.

There is less guidance here because the question is easier to decode than the previous one. What is needed here is: what the doctrine of separation of powers is (that is, that the three institutions of government – the legislature, the executive and the judiciary – are separate); how far the constitution reflects that doctrine; and how fundamental that is. Again, there is the combination of the knowledge and understanding and the cognitive and intellectual elements. As in the last question, generally the knowledge and understanding relate to the factual elements of the question and the cognitive and intellectual to the discussion of their position in the constitution.

Sample question 3

Criminal law

In *Airedale NHS Trust v Bland* the judges in the House of Lords agreed that it would be lawful for doctors to cease the treatment of Tony Bland with the result that he would die.

Discuss the extent of liability for causing death by omission.

There is a little more guidance in the second sentence here, which is necessary because the first sentence is very wide and could lead to lots of different sorts of discussion. The second sentence has narrowed the scope so that you can limit this to the circumstances in which the courts have imposed criminal liability for causing death by omission and those instances when they have not, and look at how secure and principled the line between them is. Again, knowledge and understanding and cognitive and intellectual skills are combined.

Sample question 4

Contract law

In law, a gratuitous promise is said to be unenforceable but this rule does not apply where promissory estoppel operates.

Discuss.

Here the two elements are the general rule relating to contracts and the absence of consideration, and how the principle is varied by estoppel. In this instance the knowledge and understanding required are clear but in what way are critical and intellectual skills to be employed? They are less obvious but they are there as the instruction 'discuss' is not the same as 'describe'. In looking at the rule and the exception you are expected to be critical. How clear are the exceptions provided by estoppel and how far do they mitigate the harshness of the rule, that is, make such a promise enforceable?

Decoding your question

What you need to do now is to apply these same decoding principles to your question. Firstly, what is the knowledge and understanding required? This should be fairly straightforward and the essay title should be making it clear. What is less easy to deduce are the critical and intellectual skills; they may be made explicit as in the first example but equally they may be implicit as in the others. However, as you know from the learning outcomes that they are there, you can use the examples to determine what they are in your title. What are the key words? 'Certainty' and 'flexibility' are stated in the first example but in each of the others they have had to be found. What is the key? You may have noticed that in each question there has been a dichotomy, two principles opposing each other. This is not only so in certainty and flexibility but in the separation of powers, in liability and non-liability for death by omission, and in liability on gratuitous promises and estoppel. In each title it is the key words which lead you to what the question is really asking you to do. Identify the key words in your question in the same way and you will find the answer.

Summary

This chapter has looked at:

- the purpose of essays;
- the function of learning outcomes in determining what is required of the answer;
- the application of learning outcomes to some model questions;
- and applying these lessons to your essay title.

8 Planning and Research

By the end of this chapter you should be able to:

▶ produce a timetable for working on your essay;
▶ understand how to research for an essay question;
▶ use your research to find other sources.

Timetable

The first element of planning – and the one most students forget – is a timetable. So why do you need one? The worst way to do any piece of work is to leave it until the last minute and then rush an answer which will not be very good and will not obtain the marks it ought to. Yet this is very common with student assignments because it is always tempting to put things off until you have to do them – that's human nature. There are some people who can work this way and produce something good but for most people a good essay involves taking the time to work out where the essay is going over a period of time.

The one given element governing your timetable will be the submission date. In the earlier parts of your course it is likely that your tutors will have planned the submission of assignments at intervals so that you will not have to submit several assignments over a short period of time. In later parts of your course this is less likely since a greater degree of optionality makes it more difficult, and also because one of the skills you need to learn is how to prioritise your work. (This is particularly important when it comes to producing a dissertation and we will look at this in Part 7, p. 171.) You have your submission date and you also have other work to do; even if you have no other assignment to submit before the date of the one in question you will have lectures and seminars to go to, and to prepare for. It is possible that your tutors have only given you the assignment title after you have completed the lectures and seminars relevant to it. If this is the case, you have your starting point. The alternative is that you have been given the assignment title at the beginning of your course, in which case the point at which you have had the lectures and seminars, if any, relevant to the assignment topic is your starting point. Why the qualification 'if any'? What you are more likely to find as you progress through your course is that a topic may be omitted from the taught material where it is the assignment topic, which means that you will research it yourself. This sounds frightening but by the time you reach that stage of your course you will have become so used to researching for assignments that it will not be.

Now you have a start and an end; they should rarely be less than 4 weeks apart and it is argued that this should be the minimum amount of time you should devote to an essay. What goes into the timetable? The most obvious element is writing. How long do you need to write an essay? If you allow at least a week, more if possible, that will avoid the last-minute dash. That is the end of the timetable; what about the start? You are already doing one element: reading these chapters. Once you have done what is covered in Chapter 7 you will know what the question is about and so will be able to start your research. Using what you learned from Chapter 4, you can start your research. As you read, this will produce other material so you need to make sure you allow sufficient research time. One raid of the library or search session on a database will not be enough so you need to allow a few days at least for this part of the exercise. This will then leave sufficient time to develop the structure of your essay (covered in the next chapter) and write it. If your timetable slips, and on occasions it will, do not ignore the slip but adjust your timetable to take account of it.

Researching the essay

To research for an essay, as opposed to other types of assignment, you will need to research widely, beyond textbooks and cases. Your starting point is what your tutors have given you by way of reference material. This may be just the recommended text or it may include other texts, journal articles and online materials. An essay which references only standard student texts is likely to be insufficiently academic to do more than earn a basic pass in the early stages of the course, and less later on. You want to do better. Additionally, as you go through your course your range of sources should become increasingly sophisticated. What the material you have will do is lead you to other material, specialist texts and journal articles in particular. If you look at the footnotes in most law textbooks you will see frequent references to journal articles relevant to any particular area of law. Using the skills you have learned from Chapter 4, assemble your materials. Do not forget to make sure you search the specialist law databases (see p. 26) for recent articles as book production schedules mean that new books will not have anything from the previous few months and a book a year old will probably have nothing newer than around 18 months. The same argument applies to case law. It is to be hoped that your tutors have pointed out any recent cases in the area but just in case they have not, search the case law databases for recent decisions. These searches can be extremely productive – nothing impresses a marker more than being told something they do not know.

There is one additional search you need to do for an essay: search the journals sections of the law databases using the 'author search' field to find any material written by your lecturers and tutors. As was said in Chapter 4, your lecture notes are not authoritative and should not be cited either in your essay or in the bibliography. However, published work by your lecturers and tutors is authoritative and should be cited. Although there may be students who would doubt this assertion, academics are only human and it is human nature to take pride in work which is published. If you cite such works and discuss them it is likely to pay off when the marker comes across their own work. Such items will also help you understand how members of your academic staff approach a particular area of law and so you will be able to tailor your approach in a similar way. As your critical legal skills develop in later parts of your course, you may be able to disagree with what has been written. This is what academic debate is all about and you will not lose marks for it as long as you have given the view expressed by the author proper consideration and provided the appropriate, authoritative support for your argument.

As was said in Chapter 4 (p. 32), the work of the Law Commission is extremely useful for essays. If your tutors have mentioned a Law Commission paper in respect of an area covered by your assignment, make sure you look at it. It is likely that only some parts of a Consultation Paper or Report will be relevant to your assignment and so use the index to find those parts. Your library should have paper copies of all Law Commission Consultation Papers, previously referred to as Working Papers, and Reports. Make sure you can find them. It is difficult to be prescriptive about finding Law Commission papers in law libraries as there appears not to be a consistent practice in relation to where they are shelved. Some libraries have them with Law Reports and journals, and, as these tend to be in alphabetical order, finding 'Law Commission' is easy enough. Other libraries have other shelving systems; find the one your library uses. However, it is unlikely that your library will have more than one copy of each Consultation Paper or Report so any paper relevant to an assignment may well be in demand. You can find papers since 1996 on the Law Commission's website at www.lawcom.gov.uk and older ones on the British and Irish Legal Information Institute site at http://alpha.bailii.org/openlaw/.

● Using the research

Now that you have amassed your material the most important thing is to read it as soon as it is practicable to do so. This way you can find whether the material leads you to other items that you do not have. You can then go back and find these. If you leave the detailed reading until you are due to start writing you may not have time to do this. Even if you do have the time it is likely that your less well organised colleagues are beginning to look at material by this stage, so that will make finding things more difficult.

Summary

In this chapter we have discussed:

- why a timetable of work is valuable;
- how the timetable must prevent writing in a last-minute rush and include sufficient research time;
- why it is important to provide a breadth of sources involving textbooks, cases, journal articles and online sources;
- why databases should be searched for recent articles and cases which would be unlikely to be cited in other published sources;
- the value of Law Commission Consultation Papers and Reports to essay writing.

9 Developing a Structure

By the end of this chapter you should be able to:

▶ understand the need to define the terms of your essay;
▶ apply that understanding to your question.

Answering the question

As was said in Chapter 3, what is important in an essay is that it answers the question. You will not be asked to write an essay, either as a piece of coursework or in an examination, which simply requires you to reproduce the relevant material from either your lecture notes or a textbook. So do not do it. One of the keys to avoiding reproduction is to develop a structure for your answer which makes sure that you have examined all the points relevant to the question you have been asked.

Assuming that you have decoded your question as described in Chapter 7 (pp. 72–5), you will know that the first thing you are going to need to do with an essay is to define the terms used in the question: what is the essay about? We will use the same examples:

Sample question 1

Legal method

'The rules as to precedent reflect the practice of the courts and have to be applied bearing in mind that their objective is to assist in the administration of justice. They are of considerable importance because of their role in achieving the appropriate degree of certainty as to the law. This is an important requirement of any system of justice. The principles should not, however, be regarded as so rigid that they cannot develop in order to meet contemporary needs.'

R. v Simpson [2003] EWCA Crim 1499 [27], [2004] Q.B. 118 (Lord Woolf CJ)

Discuss the above quotation with regard to certainty and flexibility within the doctrine of judicial precedent.

As discussed earlier (p. 73), the key here is how the rules as to precedent achieve a balance between certainty and flexibility. The first element therefore is what those rules of precedent actually are. This is the definition section of the 'knowledge and understanding' part of your **learning outcomes**.

Similarly, with our second example:

Sample question 2

Constitutional law

The separation of powers is a fundamental part of the constitution of the United Kingdom.

Discuss.

The first task is to state what the separation of powers is – the doctrine that the three arms of the state, the executive, the legislature and the judiciary, are separate from and independent of each other. Again, here is the knowledge element to begin with, demonstrating that you know what the question is asking you about. You can now see the pattern: that with an essay (as opposed to some other law assessments) the start is always definitional.

So, to continue the series:

Sample question 3

Criminal law

In *Airedale NHS Trust v Bland* the judges in the House of Lords agreed that it would be lawful for doctors to cease the treatment of Tony Bland with the result that he would die.

Discuss the extent of liability for causing death by omission.

As stated at p. 74, the second sentence has given the guidance needed as the first sentence is too open to define the question for you. The definition part of this question is: what are the circumstances in which the law imposes criminal liability for omissions, that is, where there is a duty? The basics of this liability you can find in your lecture notes and textbooks.

The next example was:

Sample question 4

Contract law

In law, a gratuitous promise is said to be unenforceable but this rule does not apply where promissory estoppel operates.

Discuss.

Here you do not need any further definition; the question is clear enough without it. So you can state fairly easily the basic rule of consideration in the law of contract – that if there is no consideration then the promise is unenforceable – as your starting point.

● Starting the essay

What is vital in each of these cases, and with any essay you write, is that these descriptions are short. Remember that the essence of an essay is that it is analytical, not descriptive. It is far too easy to let the descriptive take over so that you never reach the analytical part. So how do you keep it short whilst making sure that you have covered what is required? This is where two earlier lessons come in: authority and not telling stories.

The first part is *authority* (see p. 18). The standard undergraduate textbooks that have been recommended to you by your tutors will contain the information you need and provide the authority to back up what you are saying. Use their descriptions, properly referenced, of course, to define the terms of your question. You will need to go to a wider range of sources as you progress through the essay but the simplest start is often the best.

The second part is *not telling stories* (see p. 56). In most instances no case facts are required at all. If they are, a line will do. The general rule should be that you use no case facts in your essays and by developing that as a habit it will become the natural thing to do. Not only will this help with essays as coursework but the fact that you have developed this habit will help when it comes to essay questions in examinations (which we will discuss in Part 6, p. 168).

It is useful if this part of the assignment is written as early as possible, in outline at least. The reason for this is that it is easy to think when planning your research for your essay that the topic is, in the examples we used, precedent, separation of powers, murder and consideration. Those *are* the topics but, as we have seen in defining the question, it is in each case narrower than that. If you base your research on the wider topic, you will either waste time and effort because much of what you find is insufficiently specific, or your answer will be on the general area, not on the question you have been asked. If you do either you will not be doing what this book is about: achieving good marks.

Do not worry if, between the initial outline and the final piece of work you submit, the definition has changed. That is good because it means you have learned something and so the assignment has fulfilled not only its summative purpose – gaining you a mark which measures your progress – but it has also achieved its formative process as a learning tool to increase your knowledge and understanding of that area of law (see p. 4). With the possible exception of examinations, all assessments should meet both criteria, and the essay is arguably the form of assessment that meets the formative part best until you come to your final-year dissertation.

Now that the start of the essay is in place and has defined the scope of what is going to follow, the narrow research can take place concentrating on the central questions of the assignment and excluding peripheral ones. Once that is done it leads in to the main body of the essay – what it is actually about and the place where the real marks are, in analysis and criticism rather than description.

Summary

In looking at where to start with an essay this chapter has discussed:

- the definition of the assignment question and its focus;
- the value of the learning outcomes and, in particular, the value of the 'knowledge and understanding' part of them to provide the basis for the essay;
- the use of authority for the definition;
- the avoidance of case facts in order to keep the descriptive part as short as possible.

10 The Body of the Essay

By the end of this chapter you should be able to:

▶ appreciate the importance of an essay plan;
▶ construct a skeleton of an answer;
▶ fill out the skeleton from your research;
▶ test that the structure of the answer is sound.

● **Planning**

Once you have defined the terms of the question as described in the previous chapter, and you have completed, for the time being at least, your research and so have assembled material from books, cases and journal articles, the question arises of where you go from there. One answer is to start writing the rest of the essay and see how it develops – but that is not the preferred answer. The reason for that is that you are embarking on a journey with the starting point, your question, and the end point, your final answer, fairly well defined. If you start off in the general direction of the answer you will probably arrive eventually. However, in the process you are likely to go out of your way; you may become lost and have to turn back to find where you should be and the whole journey will have taken longer than it should have. You will probably have had to discard part of what you have done because it does not fit or takes you over your word limit. No matter which of these applies, they will all have one effect in common, that you have wasted time.

You may think that wasting a little time does not matter because you have organised your work so you are not running up against a deadline, your submission date. However, it does matter because of what was said in Chapter 1 (p. 4) about assignments having a formative function as well as a summative function; they are about you learning as well as about measuring what you have learned. The formative element here is of some use in many types of assignment but you can do reasonably well without it. For examinations it is invaluable. Learn this lesson now and when it comes to examinations you are already partly prepared. It is called a plan.

You are unlikely to start a journey by car to somewhere you have never been to before without planning the route, whether you use a map, satnav or both. You need the route to take you from where you are to where you want to be. It is the same with your essay. To move from your starting point to the end you need a plan, particularly as with your essay the important part is what you do on the way to the end. Most people can arrive there; the important bit is to travel well.

Developing the plan

The first piece of the plan is already in place: the definition part of your assignment. With any assessment this should not exceed about 10 per cent of your word limit, so 150 words for a 1500-word assignment and 250 for a 2500-word assignment. You may think that this is very small; it is. For comparison, this chapter has reached just under 500 words at this point.

The point of limiting the definition part of your assignment to such a small amount is, as has already been said in Chapter 9, that the key to a good assignment is to keep the descriptive piece short so that the analytical part has the vast majority of the space. The student who fills essays with descriptions from textbooks and case facts may well pass the assignment but they will not do much more.

The other end of your work is the conclusion. This should be even shorter, at about 5 per cent of your word limit: that is 75 words for a 1500-word assignment or 125 words for a 2500-word one. You do not need a long rambling conclusion since the essay itself should have made its points as it goes. The conclusion merely draws these points together to round off the essay.

That has dealt with the two end points; now your plan can cover the area in between. This will have come from your research. If you have researched the essay as was specified in Chapter 8 you will have materials from textbooks, journal articles and cases which you need to discuss. The question is, how do you put them together? The most effective way is to break the elements you wish to discuss into discrete elements. If you look at some of the journal articles you are using you will see how the argument the author is engaging in covers areas in sequence rather than lumping everything for one source together followed by another and then another. It is particularly useful if there are two contrasting arguments that you can put together to discuss the merits of each.

Skeleton

What are these elements? Going back to our examples is probably the easiest way of demonstrating what you need to do. The first was:

> ### Sample question 1
>
> *Legal method*
>
> 'The rules as to precedent reflect the practice of the courts and have to be applied bearing in mind that their objective is to assist in the administration of justice. They are of considerable importance because of their role in achieving the appropriate degree of certainty as to the law. This is an important requirement of any system of justice. The principles should not, however, be regarded as so rigid that they cannot develop in order to meet contemporary needs.'
>
> *R. v Simpson* [2003] EWCA Crim 1499 [27], [2004] Q.B. 118 (Lord Woolf CJ)
>
> Discuss the above quotation with regard to certainty and flexibility within the doctrine of judicial precedent.

In your short descriptive piece at the beginning of the essay you have said briefly what the rules of judicial precedent are, and the exceptions, those occasions when a departure from precedent is permitted. You will have discovered that the basic rules relating to departure from precedent were set down in the Court of Appeal case of *Young v Bristol Aeroplane Co. Ltd* [1944] KB 718. These have subsequently been added to by the decision of the House of Lords in 1996 to permit it to depart from its own decisions, now the position of the Supreme Court, and the more recent added exception where the earlier decision is not compatible with the Human Rights Act or a later decision in the European Court of Human Rights. This will give you five areas, which is more than enough; you may want to cut it down to three by covering the Bristol Aeroplane categories as one.

This will give you the separate parts of your assignment by enabling you to discuss each one, using the authority you have discovered in your research, in turn. As a result these areas are the skeleton of your plan. List them in the order in which you want to tackle them. That gives the basic structure of what your essay will look like.

● Structure

In order to flesh out this structure you need your research. What have judges and authors said about each of these areas and how does that relate to the search for a balance between certainty and flexibility? Add these references to your plan, juxtaposing differing views where possible, and this will give the overall structure. You are now in a position to start writing the main part of your essay. A word of warning may be appropriate here. Do not think that because you have your plan you must stick to it at all costs. If something occurs to you that will improve the outcome of your essay, be prepared to modify your plan to accommodate it. Do not just depart from the plan thinking you will come back to it; you will not. Adjust the plan to take account of the development and carry on as before.

Having the plan and sticking to it, as modified if necessary, should do the other things that are important. The first is authority: because each element of your answer is based on what you have found from a judge or author, they are your authority (see Chapter 4, p. 26). The second important element is relevance to the question you have been asked (see Chapter 2, p. 11). This will also come from your authorities but it normally needs spelling out a little more forcibly. The reason for this is that the judges and authors will not have been tackling the question you have been given so you need to point out how what they have said is relevant to your answer. As was said in Chapter 2 (p. 11), there is one guaranteed way to ensure this and that is to have the words of the question run through the answer like the word 'Blackpool' runs through a stick of rock. After each use of authority or juxtaposition, or at the end of each part of an idea, repeat the key words of the question and apply them to what you have just written.

The key words in this question are the balance between certainty and flexibility, so you can conclude each part of the discussion by saying this demonstrates how the balance between certainty and flexibility has been maintained – or that it has not. Limits on the application of exceptions may have emphasised certainty over flexibility or liberal use of the exceptions may have elevated flexibility over certainty. As long as the words are used and the authority cited, the conclusion is debatable. What is important is that you come to one, even if that conclusion is that both views are legally and intellectually defensible and that it is a matter of individual judgement as to how the outcome in any particular area is viewed.

That gives you the basis for your essay, so the other examples can be discussed more briefly. The second was:

Sample question 2

Constitutional law

The separation of powers is a fundamental part of the constitution of the United Kingdom.

Discuss.

Your introduction said what the doctrine of the separation of powers was; you can now use your research to look at individual parts. You will have discovered that there are a number of problems with the doctrine in United Kingdom constitutional law. The most important can be said to be that the Executive, the Government, is made up of members of the legislature, the House of Commons and House of Lords, and that the Prime Minister is the leader of the political party with the majority in the House of Commons. Another problem you may wish to look at is that the Attorney General is a government minister, legal adviser to the Government and responsible for consenting to prosecutions. You may wish to consider that until 2009 the highest court in the country, the House of Lords, was part of the legislature and that this ceased on the establishment of the Supreme Court. There are other areas but these are sufficient for our purposes.

Just as with the previous example, these points give the skeleton of the essay. Your research then builds the body so that you have a plan which will enable you to write the essay. You go about this in the same way as before, with the difference that many of your examples will show that the separation of powers does not apply in that instance, or that legislative changes, such as the establishment of the Supreme Court, have enhanced the separation of powers.

Similarly with the third example:

Sample question 3

Criminal law

In *Airedale NHS Trust v Bland* the judges in the House of Lords agreed that it would be lawful for doctors to cease the treatment of Tony Bland with the result that he would die.

Discuss the extent of liability for causing death by omission.

You described in your introduction that such liability only arises where there is a duty and gave instances of such a duty. Each one of these, and its limitations, can be looked at individually and this gives you your skeleton. Fill it out with what you have discovered in your research, juxtaposing views wherever possible (as demonstrated in Chapter 6, p. 55). Each part then concludes with a statement that this demonstrates the extent of liability for causing death by omission. The important part of the question is again running through the answer.

The fourth example:

Sample question 4

Contract law

In law, a gratuitous promise is said to be unenforceable but this rule does not apply where promissory estoppel operates.

Discuss.

In the introduction you have said how the law relating to consideration in the law of contract works and that promissory estoppel is an exception to this. For the main body of your work you can look at the development of estoppels as this exception and examples where it will not apply, for example to part payment of a debt. This again is your skeleton.

What you need to do now is to apply these principles to *your* question. You have decoded it, written the introductory part and assembled your materials. Now isolate the individual components which will make up the skeleton of your answer and include these in your plan, as has been done in the examples above. Fit the materials from your research round these elements to give you the body of your essay and the authority you need for the answer. Finally, ensure that you have the key words from the question to round off each element and ensure that your answer remains relevant. Then start writing. It sounds easy – and it is, once you know how and have practised a few times. It is rather like riding a bicycle. The first time you try you are convinced that you will never be able to do it; once you have learned, you rarely have to think about it because it comes to you automatically. It is the same with planning and writing assignments. Once you have got the hang of doing them the technique will feel natural. That is because it works.

● Testing the structure

How can you tell if it is working? In using authority you will have referenced what you have written, normally through footnotes (as explained in Chapter 5, pp. 38–52). If you have a structure that is juxtaposing different views, comparing and contrasting various authorities, your references will be alternating ones as you bat the discussion between authorities. If your references are lists, a large number of references to one authority followed by a large number to another, then all you are doing is describing each authority's view instead of comparing and contrasting them. If you find that a section of your essay is beginning to look descriptive in that way then go back to your plan and see how you can combine authorities rather than using them sequentially.

It may be useful, particularly if you consider you are not quite getting the knack of using authority in this way, to go back to Chapter 6 (p. 55), and look at how it was done there. Then use the same techniques in your essay. As was said at the beginning, the idea of this book is that you can go to individual sections, not necessarily whole chapters, for guidance on what you need. If you need to remind yourself of something, dip in to the relevant bit.

The other important point here is to keep checking that you are maintaining the relevance you have put in place. Do not do the checking referred to above once. Do it throughout the writing process and if you have had to go back and redo a part of your assignment because it had become too descriptive, then, when the rewriting of that section is complete, check it again. As was described in Chapter 4 (p. 26), your sources, books and journal articles have gone through a whole series of quality control procedures to ensure that they are authoritative. This is what you are aiming for. You will not achieve that level immediately as it requires a great deal of practice, and taking into account feedback from your tutors – but it is possible. The work of the very best final-year undergraduates is often of publishable standard. Keep using the techniques in this book and your work can achieve that standard.

Conclusion

Several times in this chapter conclusions have been mentioned since they are an important part of the structure of an essay. The aim of a conclusion should be to draw the various parts of the essay together. You have concluded each section of the essay using your key words; now you can pull those conclusions together, again using your key words, to answer the question as a whole. What is important is that the conclusion does draw the parts together and so builds on what is written in each section. It should not include new material which has not been used before: if it does, it is another section of the essay and not a conclusion.

In essays, as opposed to other forms of assignment, it is unlikely that a conclusion will give a definitive answer. As you progress through your degree definitive answers will become less likely rather than more likely as the questions you tackle become more complex. If there was a simple, definitive answer to the question, why would it be worth asking? Some students find this a problem. What is important to remember is that the questions you are being asked are questions on the margins of topics. In the vast majority of practical situations the straightforward answer is the right one. But in order to develop your critical skills your tutors are setting you assignments exploring the edges of the straightforward answer. As long as you explore those edges, with authority, different conclusions can be drawn and the most likely one is that opposing views are valid and it can be a matter of choice as to which is preferred.

Submission

There are a few other areas that need to be mentioned before leaving the topic of essays. The first, and one of the most important, is that an essay should be a single piece of work. As a result it should not have section headings. This book has chapter titles and subheads to enable you to dip into it at relevant points; an essay is not for dipping into but for reading as a whole. Headings belong in reports and you may have friends on other degree courses where they have to write reports. Unless you are doing law with another subject you are unlikely to be asked to do so. That is why there is no Reports section in this book.

Additionally, remember what was said in Chapter 6 about English. Tutors often receive work from students in which, in an attempt to use sophisticated language, they have misused words or used complex words where simple ones are better. This is a problem that is found particularly in essays. The answer is simple: do not do it. If you are not sure about this go back to the section of Chapter 6 (pp. 58–65), where this is discussed.

The final thing to do with your essay is to ensure you submit it. This may appear a silly thing to say but students frequently complete work and then think that, rather than submitting it immediately, they will wait until the final submission date. This is a bad idea because if something then goes wrong you will not have time to put it right. If you submit a paper copy of your essay, make sure you print it before the deadline day; if you submit electronically, post the electronic copy before deadline day. Failure to submit on time, without permission, usually produces a penalty. An example is that an essay up to a week late qualifies for a maximum mark of 40 per cent; if it is more than a week late it qualifies for 0 per cent! You have not put in all that effort to achieve marks like that – but you will be unlikely to receive permission to submit late just because your computer developed a fault or your printer ran out of ink. Avoid the problem and you will not have to solve it.

Summary

In this chapter we have looked at:

- the practical aspects of writing law essays;
- the definition part of the answer, the plan and applying it, and the conclusion;
- why the definition part of the answer is limited to 10 per cent of the word count;
- how the essay develops from the definition to a skeleton of ideas to being fleshed out with the research material by comparing and contrasting views;
- techniques for testing if the aim of an analytical essay has been achieved;
- the function of a conclusion;
- a few simple tips about headings, language and submission.

Part 3

Problem Questions

11 Why Do We Do Them?

By the end of this chapter you should be able to:

▶ appreciate why problem questions are set;
▶ identify, define, explain and apply;
▶ use timelines to determine the nature of the problem;
▶ differentiate between major and minor questions.

Introduction to problem solving

The problem question is a widely used vehicle for testing the knowledge and understanding of the law student. To those who have never come across them before they may, at first, seem daunting. Usually they involve dispensing advice to one or more imaginary **claimant**s or **defendant**s. It is this advising that often leads students to make their first mistake: failure to ignore reality.

When your tutor asks you to 'Advise X', he or she does not want you to advise them to see a solicitor, for example. Practical issues such as obtaining legal aid are also usually irrelevant. You are instead being asked to consider the legal issues raised by the question and apply the law to the given set of facts before you.

This is not what a solicitor or other legal adviser would do in practice because the vast majority of clients would not understand the legal terms being used, nor would they want the level of detail you are being asked to give. The nature of the exercise is more like the questions such an adviser would ask themselves and the answers that they would provide to those questions. The job of the problem question is, then, to allow students to demonstrate that they can effectively identify legal issues from a given scenario; to show that they can sort the relevant from the irrelevant; and to demonstrate that they understand the application of the statutory provisions and legal principles derived from case law that they have learned about in particular contexts.

Although it is important to be concise and precise in what you say, it is also important that you use the opportunity of answering the question to demonstrate the knowledge that you have acquired in the area concerned to the marker. When students first start to answer this type of question, the answers that they produce are often only one or two paragraphs long. Although the kernel of an answer may be found within such a short response, in order to acquire better marks expansion is required.

Some law tutors help students to achieve the task of answering problem-style questions more fully, and therefore effectively, by referring to the acronym IDEA: **I**dentify, **D**efine, **E**xplain (or sometimes Expand or Evaluate) and **A**pply.

The first stage of answering the question, therefore, requires you to identify the legal issues with which the problem question is concerned. So for example:

Sample question 1

Contract law

Anne is a regular customer at her local pub, the King's Arms. Anne offers to decorate the upstairs rooms in the pub. Upon completion of the job, Brenda, the landlady of the King's Arms, is so delighted with the result of Anne's work that she agrees to pay her £500 in appreciation of her efforts. However, the following week Brenda informs Anne that she has changed her mind because she cannot afford to pay her the £500.

Advise Anne.

This question is concerned with the doctrine of consideration in contract.

It is common practice in some modules for questions of this type to deal with only one area of knowledge. For example, in a Level (or year) 1 Law of Contract module, each question you are asked, whether it be in a tutorial or seminar setting, as an in-course assessment or as part of an examination, might focus on just one topic from the module. In other modules, for example on a Criminal Law course, each question might require consideration of two or more of the areas, for example a substantive offence such as murder and the liability of not only the murderer but of others who have been involved in committing the offence. You will have studied these as separate topics on your Criminal Law course but will be required to combine them for the assessment. Your tutors should be able to give you advice as to this issue in relation to their module.

The second task is to 'define' the area with which the problem is concerned. This might involve defining what is meant by the name of the topic. For example, 'consideration' in the law of contract could be explained by reference to definitions provided in the judgments of cases (a primary source) and also by considering the views of academic authors as set out in textbooks (a secondary source). Obviously reference to the former rather than the latter is more authoritative but the second will often add to your answer, if only in that it will explain what the judges in the relevant cases meant in a more accessible way. You might also at this stage wish to make other introductory remarks; for example, with respect to consideration, you could briefly outline its role in the law of contract and perhaps even make an aside as to fact that most other legal systems do not require it. Be careful not to go too far down this road, however (see Chapter 6, p. 54, where this is discussed in more detail). Sometimes a couple of lines are all that is needed in this regard. It is important to make sure that you keep what you say relevant to the question.

The next thing to do is explain the legal material that is relevant to the question. This is often best achieved by explaining the law that relates to each point raised by the scenario and simultaneously applying (the fourth stage) this to the given facts. For example:

Sample answer 1

Past consideration is said to be no consideration (*Roscorla v Thomas*; *Re McArdle*). This means that acts done in the past cannot be consideration for later promises. Here, Brenda makes a promise to Anne that she will pay her £500. This promise comes after Anne has carried out the act in respect of which the promise is made. It would appear then that, *prima facie*, the promise is unenforceable.

Sometimes students prefer to write out all of the information that they know in relation to a particular topic and then apply it to the question. This is a high-risk strategy, in terms of achieving a high mark, for a number of reasons. First, students who adopt this approach often run out of time (in an exam situation) or words (in the production of an assignment) and end up not applying what they have said to the question at all. The main learning outcome that is applicable in answering problem questions is:

Identify the relevant legal issues in hypothetical problems of limited complexity and apply those principles in arriving at arguable conclusions.

This will be almost impossible to meet if all you do is simply write out the relevant law. Whilst you may get some credit for doing this you will not achieve a good mark (see Chapter 2, p. 11).

The second risk with this approach is that you will forget to apply what is said to each point raised by the scenario. Often students will write out several pages of law followed by just a couple of paragraphs of application. If you apply the law to the facts as you go along you cannot leave something important out.

The third risk is that your answer could contain a lot of irrelevant material. As we said in the essay part of this book, you will never find a question that asks you simply to write out everything you know about a particular topic. Problem questions require, in the same way that essays do, focus on a certain area or areas. In some ways, they are even more specific as they involve application of the law to an exact set of facts.

The fourth risk is that you may end up repeating yourself in an effort to address what has been said to the facts of the scenario.

The nature of the question

Different styles of problem question demand different types of response. We will give you some advice as to how each type should be tackled. At first you may feel that it is difficult to know which approach is required when, but with practice you will develop in confidence. This is where your tutorial/seminar programme is invaluable.

Particularly in the earlier parts of a law degree, the tutorial/seminar programmes that most tutors design for their modules focus heavily on answering problem-style questions, so you should have plenty of opportunities to tackle this type of work before you need to do it in assessment situations. Use these chances to your advantage. For every tutorial cycle, in advance of the session, prepare an answer to the question. Some tutors may even be happy to look at these and tell you if you are taking the right approach.

Problem questions have usually been drafted in such a way that the facts used are reminiscent of those of decided cases. Often part of a scenario will focus on, for example, two cases that can be distinguished from one another.

Some questions will be very specific and others may leave some issues deliberately vague. In questions that do not contain all of the necessary details to provide a definitive answer on a particular matter, it is open to you to speculate (within the realms of reasonableness) as to what might happen if situation A or situation B were the case. For example, looking back to the consideration question referred to above, one factor that the courts will consider in relation to the exceptions to the rule against past consideration is whether there was an expectation that the party would be rewarded for their act. You might speculate here then as to reasons that might have created that expectation in Anne and conversely reasons why Brenda might not have expected to pay. However, as we have said: do not take this too far. Do not speculate what might happen if Anne were a Martian or something equally ridiculous. You are engaging in this exercise simply to show the marker that you are aware that different factors may have an influence on the outcome of the advised party's case.

Where questions are specific, you should not try to vary the facts as they are presented. If, for example, a criminal law question tells you that the two potential defendants are minors or that they are best friends, there is a reason for this and you do not need to discuss what the situation would be if they were not.

● **Alternative instructions**

If, instead of 'Advise X', the question asks you to discuss the legal issues raised by this question, the approach needs to vary. This style of question presents you with more of an obvious opportunity to depart from the close facts of the scenario and bring in the views of academics on the particular legal point under discussion by referring to journal articles and books. It is common to find this instruction attached to questions asked in modules studied later in your law degree programme. This is because the **learning outcomes** at that level tend to require more depth of analysis and evaluation than is required of students at the beginning of their studies and so tutors will often include this sort of question to provoke this. When you answer these questions, rather than simply applying the law to the scenario as the issues present themselves, the marker is asking you to analyse and comment on the law with which the scenario is concerned. You need to make sure you do this, as treating these questions in exactly the same way as 'Advise' questions will restrict the mark that you are awarded.

Report-style questions are also sometimes used by tutors. As the name suggests, these require the production of a report for a named individual as to the application of the law to a given scenario, in much the same way as a traditional problem. Differences between this type of question and the more usual style of problem may, however, be apparent in that sometimes report questions include more precise facts (and therefore allow for less discussion of particular issues) or request more specific advice, sometimes in the form of a response to one or more detailed questions. What is almost certain to be different so far as these questions are concerned is your response to them. Reports, unlike answers to other types of law question where they are heavily discouraged, require the use of headings and subheadings.

● Timelines

One aspect of the scenarios that are set for problem questions is that they normally involve a sequence of events rather than a single isolated incident. This has two important consequences. Firstly, the sequence can help with the structure of your answer and this is covered in the next chapter. Secondly, and probably more valuably, the sequence points you to the answer. For this reason it is vital that you do not speculate as to what the result might have been if the sequence of events had been different, as this will change the nature of the question.

Here is another contract example:

Sample question 2

Contract law

Wrecking Crew Builders plc was hired by Fulchester United FC to construct a new training ground. The work was to be completed by September 5th. By August 20th, after holding a meeting with Wrecking Crew, the directors of Fulchester were worried that the work would not be completed on time. Consequently they offered a £10,000 bonus to the builders if the work was completed by September 5th. Upon completion of the work Fulchester refused to pay the £10,000 bonus.

Advise the parties.

It is the fact that the bonus was offered subsequent to the contract being entered into that makes this a question about the nature of consideration. If the timing of the offer was before the contract was entered into, it would make the question one about the terms of the contract (do they include the bonus or not?), and if it were a slightly different statement that induced Wrecking Crew Builders to enter into the contract (but was not in the contract and was not true), it would be a question on misrepresentation. Do not worry if you do not know what these terms mean yet; you will be able to find them in your contract syllabus.

Remember: if you change the timeline you will not be addressing the question you have been asked so will not get the sort of marks you are looking for.

● Major questions and minor questions

In answering a problem question it is important to appreciate that not all parts of the question are of equal importance. If there is only one part to the question this is not a problem but if there are two or more, as there will be as you progress through your course and the questions you are set become more complex, then you will need to look at the relative weight to be given to each part of the answer. For example, in the case of the criminal law question we mentioned earlier:

> A question might require consideration of two or more of the areas, for example a substantive offence such as murder and the liability of not only the murderer but of others who have been involved in committing the offence.

It is likely that the major question concerns the substantive offence and the minor question the liability of others.

This is not inevitable. It is perfectly possible for the substantive offence to be the minor part and the involvement of others the major one. In order to determine which of these possibilities applies it is necessary to examine the question itself. In general, if more material in the question relates to one part of the problem, that is likely to be the major part. Similarly, if the material relating to each part is more or less equal, it is likely that that is the balance required in the answer. Sometimes, particularly in exam questions, tutors will designate marks for each part so showing which is the major and which the minor, or, if the marks are equal, that the two parts are of equal weight.

Summary

In this chapter we have identified that:

- a problem question is aimed at producing an answer to a hypothetical scenario in which the student examines the problem and answers it with legal authority from case law, statute and secondary sources;
- the answer can be achieved by applying IDEA: Identify, Define, Explain, Apply;
- the problem is tackled throughout the answer so as to meet the relevant learning outcome;

- in most instances the instruction is to advise, but wider issues can be addressed with alternative instructions;
- the key to the question is the timeline which defines the nature of the question;
- some problem questions address a single issue but others relate to two or more and the balance of the answer should reflect the balance of the question.

12 Planning and Research

By the end of this chapter you will be able to:

▶ plan an answer to a problem question;
▶ construct a skeleton answer;
▶ identify appropriate sources;
▶ research the problem.

Structure

Structure is all-important in dealing with a problem question. As we have said before, if you do not consider your structure you may end up missing something out of your answer or, worse still, not answering the question at all but simply writing out your notes on that particular topic. The latter will gain you few marks.

Many students prefer to answer problem-style questions as they believe that they are 'easier' to do than writing an essay. Whilst tackling problems should not be any more difficult than producing a response to a standard essay-style question (certainly with practice and following some of the advice that is dispensed here), that they are easier is simply not true. Answering problems effectively, as with answering other styles of question, merely requires an application of the relevant set of skills.

So why do some students think that problem questions are easier? It appears to be because the question seems to flag up the relevant areas that need to be considered and leads you through the area under consideration. This is indeed helpful to the student and will probably assist most of those who are familiar with the subject matter of the question to achieve a pass mark. However, most students are not satisfied with that (and neither should they be). How, then, do you take your answer from a pass to an excellent response? To the extent that this is possible to explain, there are at least some strategies that students can employ in an effort to do this.

Planning

Perhaps the most important strategy – and one that is often overlooked – is the production of a plan. It is often said that 'to fail to plan is to plan to fail', and this can be seen in the answers that are produced by some students when presented with problem questions. The most common answers that exhibit this approach are the 'write everything you know' or 'scattergun' approach answers. Very rarely (if at all) will a problem question require you to consider all aspects of the particular topic under consideration, and certainly you will never come across questions that merely require you to regurgitate your notes (see above). Problem questions tend to focus on particular issues. As we have said before, these may be issues where the cases are inconsistent or distinctions between the decisions are very narrowly drawn or where the law is unclear. The answer that you give needs to reflect this. A plan will help.

In our experience students (strangely) tend to be more likely to produce a plan when producing an in-course assessment than when they are in an exam. It seems that they think plans are a good idea, because when we discuss producing them when we are practising answering problems in tutorials/seminars there is much nodding of heads, but what happens between this and the exam room? Generally speaking, the answer appears to be 'panic'. It would seem that as soon as some students see other (often worse-prepared) students scribbling away furiously, all notions of writing a plan go out of the window! Our advice? Take a deep breath, ignore everyone else and spend 5 well-invested minutes of your exam time writing a plan. It will pay dividends and may, in fact, save you time in the long run. This is dealt with in more detail in Part 6 (see p. 169).

So what are the benefits of producing a plan? Obviously, there are some differences between exams and in-course assessments in this regard but, that said, plans are clearly useful for the preparation of both.

We have already said that they stop you from writing everything you know and that, as a consequence, they save you time because you are not wasting it discussing irrelevant issues. In the context of an in-course assessment, 'time' can be replaced with 'words'. Generally, part of the test of answering any question, but specifically a problem-style one, is being concise and therefore students are required to complete their assignments within a fairly tightly drawn word limit. Cutting out the superfluous material from your work by drawing up a plan will give you more words to use for the discussion of the relevant issues.

Drawing up a plan tends to make you read the question more carefully. It gives you the chance to pick out all of the relevant issues before you start writing and thereby improves the structure of your work. If you just dive straight in to answering the question, again, time can be wasted when you realise that you have been researching or writing about an irrelevant issue (if you do realise). In assignments or in seen exams, a plan will enable you to engage in research more effectively because you will have already started to pick out the relevant legal issues. Compare, for example, the number of journal articles returned on a database search for 'consideration' with the number on the more restricted search 'past consideration'.

In an exam setting, planning gives you a chance to pull yourself together if you do happen to be nervous. It makes you pause and reflect, which will hopefully lead to a better answer. Contrary to what many students think, the rule with respect to exam answers is generally not 'the longer, the better'. Three pages of relevant material, supported by authority, carefully considered and applied in detail to the question are worth much more than a 10-page stream of consciousness. A plan also enables you to look at all the events happening in a question and prevents you from going down a particular avenue only to find that a later fact in the scenario means that that issue is not relevant.

An added bonus with planning answers in exams is that there is an opportunity at the beginning of the test to note down all the material that is relevant to answering the question. Often once students commence writing their answer they become lost in the detail of what they are writing and consequently when they come to consider later parts of the scenario they forget the law/main cases that relate to them. It is also true that, if you run out of time in the exam, some tutors will give you credit for the material in the plan if it is clear what you would have written to finish an answer.

● The skeleton

So how will you structure your plan? If we return to IDEA – Identify, Define, Explain, Apply – this will give the basis for the plan. However, although in general you would 'Identify' initially, the other aspects of the acronym are applied to the various stages of the problem sequentially rather than each being completed for the whole scenario.

The first part of your plan is to identify the subject area of the problem question. What is it about? To return to our earlier example in Chapter 11:

Sample question 2

Contract law

Wrecking Crew Builders plc was hired by Fulchester United FC to construct a new training ground. The work was to be completed by September 5th. By August 20th, after holding a meeting with Wrecking Crew, the directors of Fulchester were worried that the work would not be completed on time. Consequently they offered a

> £10,000 bonus to the builders if the work was completed by September 5th. Upon completion of the work Fulchester refused to pay the £10,000 bonus.
>
> Advise the parties.

'Identify', as was said earlier, is that the question is about consideration in contract and, in particular, later consideration for an earlier promise.

'Define' will enable you to state what consideration is and what the later consideration for the performance of an existing duty is.

'Explain' in this context is to explain the law on each point raised in the scenario and 'Apply' at the same time to the facts you have been given. So here you could begin to 'Explain' and 'Apply' by stating the general rule that where a party to a contract is under a duty to perform that contract he cannot enforce a later promise to pay extra money for no additional duty. You then repeat 'Explain' and 'Apply' for each subsequent part of the answer. In this example it would be looking at exceptions to the general rule and how they apply to this scenario. You will finish with a conclusion which will be the actual advice you have been asked to give.

Filling the skeleton

Once you have your skeleton you can fill it out with authority from cases and secondary sources such as textbooks that you have discovered in your research, as explained in Chapter 4 (p. 26). If you need a reminder, go back and look at it again. This will give you something with which you can start writing the assignment itself.

Sources

Often the most useful starting point for producing the answer to a problem question will be your lecture and tutorial or seminar notes. These should help you to identify the cases and statutes that you will need to refer to. This will almost certainly be the situation in the earlier parts of your course, although later on in your programme you may be asked to produce work on areas that you have not dealt with in taught sessions. In that instance you will need to identify the relevant primary sources (cases and legislation) yourself. This is often not as daunting as it may sound, and usually reading a relevant chapter in a textbook will give you a start. However, sometimes more in-depth research may be required, but with the increased availability of specialist law databases this is also not too difficult to carry out (see Chapter 4, p. 31).

Once you have identified the relevant cases and statutes, it is often very helpful to read the judgments and the statutory provisions in full. Of course you can read what learned academics think about what these say in text-books, but there is sometimes no substitute for doing the groundwork your-self. For example, you may pick up something useful from a **dissenting judgment** in a case that may improve your answer, or you may find that a very recent enactment that has not been considered in the most up-to-date text has had an effect on a piece of legislation. In time you will acquire the skill of doing this more quickly as you become more used to sorting the rele-vant from the irrelevant, so try not to be put off if your first attempt seems to involve a lot of work. You are not wasting time: you are working on your assessment.

Some students – and indeed some tutors – consider that most of the authority when answering problem questions will be derived from primary sources and whilst to some extent this is true, with such questions providing a useful opportunity to consider, for example, contrasting judgments in detail, primary sources should not be relied upon to the exclusion of all others.

There is scope for reference to textbooks as authority for general asser-tions and definitions as well as a location for 'further reading' advice in their bibliographies and footnotes, where you will find citations for a whole variety of more specialist texts and journal articles.

Students often ask how they can employ journal articles when producing answers to problem questions. The advice is much the same here as that relating to the production of other forms of in-course work: in other words, journal articles should be used for opinion and argument to support your answer. For example, if the problem question involves consideration of a problematic line of case law, learned authors must have different opinions as to how difficulties in that area should be resolved, and these could be brought into your answer as suggested solutions advocated by the writers in question.

Summary

This chapter has:

- identified that the key is structure;
- examined the structure of the problem question;

- determined that the plan must avoid the scattergun approach;
- shown how the plan draws the answer much closer to the question, concentrates on relevant topics and helps avoid irrelevancies;
- shown how secondary sources such as textbooks and journal articles are also valuable in pointing to solutions.

13 Developing a Structure

By the end of this chapter you should be able to:

▶ structure the answer to a problem question using the IDEA acronym;
▶ appreciate how identification and definition form the basis of the answer;
▶ understand how to explain and apply in relation to each element of the problem;
▶ identify when a partial problem only requires certain parts of an answer;
▶ value a conclusion;
▶ test the answer from the referencing.

Starting the answer

In our experience, one of the most difficult things about writing a problem answer is actually putting pen to paper, or fingers to keyboard. You have identified the relevant legal issues and you have investigated these further through your research – but how do you use this information to construct an answer? Where do you start? The question asks you to 'Advise X'. What does this require in practice?

If we return to the IDEA acronym, the best place to start would appear to be with an identification of the relevant topic under discussion. So for example, you may say in response to an EU Law question:

> This question concerns the free movement of goods.

or, in response to a Law of Contract question:

> This question concerns the doctrine of consideration.

It can be as straightforward as that.

There are several ways in which it is best *not* to start your answer. As mentioned in Chapter 11 (p. 95), these questions should not be answered by students pretending to be solicitors, so you do not need to set your 'advice' out in the form of a letter and you do not need to make opening remarks with respect to Legal Aid, etc. You should also not start your response to the question with a single sentence setting out your conclusion, e.g. 'Yes, X can successfully sue Y.' We have, in the past, seen this sentence as the whole answer to a question! Although you might have been encouraged at other times in your education to begin your answer by explaining what you are going to do and how you are going to do it, this is not appropriate either. What we mean by this is that a good answer would not begin:

> I am going to advise x about y. In doing so I am going to look at a, b and c, I am going to explain those concepts with reference to decided cases and then I am going to apply what I have said to the question.

A tutor's response to that will be: 'Good, because that is what you have been asked to do – but just do it!'

To demonstrate, we can go back to a simple example we used in Chapter 11:

Sample question 1

Contract law

Anne is a regular customer at her local pub, the King's Arms. Anne offers to decorate the upstairs rooms in the pub. Upon completion of the job, Brenda, the landlady of the King's Arms, is so delighted with the result of Anne's work that she agrees to pay her £500 in apprecia-tion of her efforts. However, the following week Brenda informs Anne that she has changed her mind because she cannot afford to pay her the £500.

Advise Anne.

Definition of the area with which the question is concerned can often be achieved relatively easily but sometimes, if the area is ill defined, contentious or problematic, this can present another opportunity to compare and contrast case law and to bring in the views of authors. For example, with respect to a question concerned with the consideration there are a number of definitions of that doctrine provided for by case law, in particular those given in *Currie v Misa* and *Dunlop v Selfridge*. Much has been written that crit-icises the *Currie* definition and compares it unfavourably with the *Dunlop* one. This discussion can be brought into your answer and can be applied to the facts. For example, the definition in *Currie* talks of consideration in terms of one party to a contract receiving a benefit and the other suffering a detri-ment whereas the *Dunlop* definition recognises that benefit *and* detriment may occur on both sides of the agreement. Relating this to the example, you might say:

Sample answer 1

The *Currie* definition may be demonstrated by the fact that if Brenda pays Anne the £500, Brenda has the detriment (she no longer has the £500 she had) and Anne gets the benefit (she now has the £500). However, the *Dunlop* definition takes this further in that Anne has the benefit of the £500 and the detriment of having done the work whereas Brenda has the benefit of having the pub redecorated and the detriment of having paid the £500.

You could even bring wider discussions into your answer if you do this sufficiently carefully. For example, you could when explaining the notion of consideration and how in English law its presence is necessary to render contracts legally enforceable, mention the fact that it is not found in other legal systems and that the doctrine as a whole has been criticised by judges and academic commentators alike. What you need to be careful of here, though, is that you do this in just a couple of thoughtfully crafted lines referenced to relevant authority. Whilst it is important to show the tutor who is assessing your work that you have a feel for the area as a whole, the most important thing is that you actually address the problem itself. Reference to academic debate is merely the icing on the cake.

Other bonus points can be scored for mentioning legal system type of information. For example, reference to the value of a long-standing House of Lords' precedent or conflicting Court of Appeal decisions in a particular area will add value to your answer.

The body of the answer

In terms of the 'Explaining/Expanding/Evaluating' and 'Applying' stages, depending on the style of question asked these are often most effectively dealt with if they are tackled together. The best way to keep to a structure in answering problem-style questions is to deal with the issues as they arise (your plan will also help with this, see Chapter 12, p. 105). It is often useful to look at each line of the question and to consider why that line is there. There is usually a reason for the inclusion of at least every line in a problem scenario, and sometimes every word. Some lines may set the scene, whereas others will include essential facts and others still may contain information that may colour your view of the surrounding lines. Returning to the Anne and Brenda example, for instance, the statement that Anne is a regular customer at the pub may seem irrelevant but it could demonstrate a previous relationship or discussions between the parties about the decorating or the landlady knowing the customer was a painter and decorator.

In order to answer the question fully you need to make sure that you are constantly focused on what it is that you are being asked. It is easy to stray from the point once you start to set out the law relating to a particular area, so one way of ensuring that you are not doing this is to regularly refer back to the facts of the scenario. For example, in the consideration question that we referred to earlier, there was an issue related to past consideration. Once you have identified and defined consideration and explained that the question in particular relates to past consideration, use the scenario itself for your examples. What we mean by this is that there is no need, in an answer to a question that relates to an act involving decorating that may or may not amount to consideration, to say 'If X mowed Y's lawn last week and Y offers to reward him after the event the act of mowing the lawn is past consideration.' You have a scenario with facts in it in front of you: why invent more? This reference back to the facts will ensure that you are applying what you have written to the facts of the scenario and will also ensure that you follow your plan. In other words, like the 'Blackpool' through the stick of rock analogy that we referred to in essay writing, repeated references back to the facts of the scenario will show that you are applying what you have said to the question and will make sure that you answer the question. If significant passages of your work do not mention the hypothetical problem, it seems likely that you are no longer producing an answer to a problem-style question but an essay on a related topic.

You will also need to be selective within the sub-areas raised by the questions. By this we mean that if the question is about past consideration you still should not write out all of your notes on that area in order to provide an answer. The scenario, through its facts, will point you in the direction of one part of that part of a topic. For example, the question might concern the exceptions to the general rule on past consideration. This then would be your focus. Whilst you would need to set out the rule against past consideration, you would concentrate your attentions on the exceptions and applying what you said about those (supported by case authority) to the facts of the scenario.

This is the part of your answer where you might like to make reference to contrasting cases. It is useful, therefore, to look not just at what textbook writers say about decisions but to look at the primary sources yourself and compare and contrast the material facts (see Chapter 6, p. 55).

● Part problems

Although the general approach using the IDEA acronym works well with whole problems, there are times, particularly in the first year of a law degree, when you might be asked to tackle just a small part of a problem. For example, this would be a fairly typical question in criminal law:

Sample question: part problem

Identify the *mens rea* and *actus reus* in respect of each of the following cases:

(a) ...
(b) ...
(c) ...
(d) ...

Because of the nature of the question you are not being asked to **I**dentify the legal issues involved as you would be in a full problem: the issues have been identified for you in the question. Equally, you are not being asked to **D**efine those issues since the question does not require you to define what the *mens rea* and *actus reus* of a criminal offence are. You are also not being asked to **E**xplain, because you cannot do that without at least some elements of the previous parts. What you are being asked to do is **A**pply the given identification to each of the scenarios you have been given. In this case that is what you should do.

In answering this type of question, students are frequently tempted to do the things they have not been asked for. This is the kind of introduction to the answer that is commonly encountered in student work in answer to one of these partial problems:

Sample answer: part problem

The *mens rea* of a criminal offence is the mental element of that offence: what intention, recklessness or other mental state is required for the offence to be committed. A mental element is a necessary component of all criminal offences other than those of strict liability.

The *actus reus* of an offence is the act or omission which the offender has committed which is the basis of the criminal offence.

In order for a person to be found guilty of a criminal offence, not only must the *mens rea* and the *actus reus* both be present but they must coincide; that is, they must both be present at the same time.

As a statement of the law, this is unexceptional and in a more general question it might be something you would write, obviously adding authority for your statements. However, if you have been asked a partial question such as the one given earlier, such an introduction would gain no marks because it is not what you have been asked to do. As a result, do not do it. Answer the question you have been set.

Conclusions

Whilst a conclusion is important, in that you do not want your tutor to think that the last page of your work has gone astray, the conclusion does not always have to be a definitive one. Although sometimes the question that you are asked may allow for a black or white 'answer' to the advisee's problem, it may also be the case that the scenario with which you are concerned contains insufficient detail in terms of factors that could affect the outcome, or that the law in the area in which the question is asked may be insufficiently clear to allow for such a conclusion. In these circumstances your conclusion may be one that simply summarises what you have said in the answer that precedes the final paragraph. This in itself can be useful as it will require you to look back through your answer in an effort to create the summary and through this process you can ensure that you have dealt with all of the relevant issues.

In more complex questions, or those at a higher level where more than one topic is dealt with in a scenario, it is also useful to consider more general matters such as remedies in the concluding paragraphs of your answer. This will show your tutor that you have a grasp of the wider issues involved in the module and is often particularly important in practical subjects such as the Law of Consumer Protection and questions concerning the application of the fundamental freedoms in EU law.

Referencing

Just as with essays, the referencing of your problem question will inform your answer. If your footnotes are a string of references to one source followed by a string of references to another, you are describing rather than analysing. If your footnotes show sequential sources – one case, then another, then possibly a textbook or journal article source – then you can be fairly confident you are doing it correctly. One way the referencing for a problem question will differ from that for an essay is that the balance of sources will have changed to a greater reliance on primary sources (cases and statutes), and a lesser reliance on secondary sources (textbooks and journal articles). As we said earlier, this does not mean you ignore secondary sources but that they take a less prominent place than they would in most other law assessments.

Summary

This chapter has covered how:

- the structure is developed through the elements of the IDEA acronym;
- identification of the area covered is the starting point of answers;
- definition looks at the legal consequences of the facts in the scenario;
- explanation and application follow serially (with the scenario running through the answer like 'Blackpool' through a stick of rock) and include looking at contrasting cases and the views of authors;
- a conclusion draws together what has gone before and may be definitive but need not be;
- the sequence of footnotes should show the use of a progression of different sources.

Part 4

Presentations

14 Why Are They Different?

By the end of this chapter you should be able to:

▶ appreciate the functions of presentations;
▶ understand how they differ from other assessments;
▶ appreciate questions of scale;
▶ apply these lessons to your presentation.

The purpose of presentations

The answer to the question of why presentations are different involves examining the function of presentations: what are they there for? One answer is that it is difficult to call yourself a lawyer if you cannot stand up and speak. Go into any court and you will see that this is what the lawyers are doing – so one function of a presentation is presentation itself. You may think that you are not going into advocacy, either as a barrister or a solicitor, and so you do not need it. However, whatever path you decide to follow in your subsequent career you are likely to need to present in some form or other, to a client, a class or colleagues.

The other principal function relates to the content of the presentation. With an essay or problem question as a piece of coursework, you can revise the piece of work until you are satisfied it is as good as you can make it. In a presentation, although you will prepare thoroughly, you only have one attempt to communicate your ideas to your audience. There are no second attempts. These two functions can be considered separately, but always remember that it is their combination which is important.

The best way to look at the presentation function is to examine what you are being asked to do – this you will find in your **learning outcomes** under 'transferable skills'. If you do not have these, use the ones provided in the Appendix: there are two sets, one for an oral presentation and one for a poster presentation. You may also be given the templates which your tutors use to mark the presentation. If you have these, use them, but in case you do not have them two are included in Appendix 1, again one for an oral presentation (p. 193) and one for a poster presentation (p. 196). These will be considered in detail later. For now, the concentration will be on oral presentations.

⬤ The oral presentation

The one thing a presentation is not, is reading an essay. There are two principal reasons for this: one is about authority and the other about scale. In an essay you use your authority from cases, textbooks, journal articles and other sources, referenced by footnotes. If you are doing a presentation the audience cannot hear the footnotes. This means that for the audience to understand that you are using authority, the authority must be clear from what you have said. Students frequently appear to find this difficult and so they fail to do it, yet, as with many things covered in this book, once you get used to doing it, it is quite easy.

In an essay you might write:

> Some authors consider that self-determination in medical law, although it has increased over recent years, should be taken further to embrace actively bringing about death[1] whilst others consider that autonomy has gone too far and other values should be taken into account.[2]

Or you might have written:

> Powell[1] considers that self-determination in medical law, although it has increased over recent years, should be taken further to embrace actively bringing about death, whilst Smith[2] responds that autonomy has gone too far and other values should be taken into account.

The footnotes would then provide the authority for these statements. In a presentation, this authority comes into the main body of the work. Examples might be:

> **Example 1: presentation answer**
>
> Powell in his article 'Whose Life Is It Anyway? Law and Autonomy in Choosing Death' considers that although self-determination in medical law has increased in recent years it should be taken further to embrace actively bringing about death. However, Smith in her response argues that autonomy has gone too far and that other values should be taken into account.

This communicates the authority to your audience just as the footnotes would to the reader of the essay.

Where your authority is a primary source this is less of a problem as the same format will work in an essay or a presentation. To use an example given earlier:

Example 2: presentation answer

In *Airedale NHS Trust v Bland* the judges in the House of Lords agreed that it would be lawful for doctors to cease the treatment of Tony Bland with the result that he would die. However, the route by which they reached this conclusion differed. Lord Goff considered that the solution lay in the proposition that the right of self-determination should not be lost by virtue of incompetence. This is approaching, but not quite reaching, a substitute decision test: that is, making the decision the judge believes the patient would have made if he had been capable. Lord Browne-Wilkinson, on the other hand, said that the duty to provide treatment to the incompetent patient ended when the treatment ceased to be of benefit to the patient. Moreover, he said that at that point to continue treatment would be unlawful.

This would be fine in either an essay or a presentation; the authority is there.

However, the analogy of putting your footnotes into what you say must not be taken too far, as it unfortunately sometimes is. In the first example your footnotes would look something like this:

1. D P Powell 'Whose Life Is It Anyway? Law and Autonomy in Choosing Death' (2008) Any Law Journal 211.
2. E L Smith 'Whose Life Is It Anyway? A Response' (2009) Any Law Journal 52.

Do not be tempted to put all this information in the body of the presentation because it appears clumsy and breaks up the argument. Only use enough, as in the examples given, to communicate the authority.

● The scale of a presentation

The other distinguishing point about presentations is about scale: although a presentation may contain as many words as an essay, the scope is normally much smaller. Typically, an essay would cover an area but a presentation would cover one case. Frequently students, because they are used to writing essays, see the presentation in the same way. As has been shown, that is not so. The most common statement tutors hear from students when proposing a presentation topic is: 'I want to do a presentation on X.' The tutor's response to this is likely to be: 'What about X?'

If the answer is 'I don't know', or more often 'Just about it', then the student is starting from the wrong place. The point of a presentation, as with other forms of assessment, is to provide an analysis of something, not a commentary. If your tutor has spent an hour in a lecture on a topic, you are not going to do that topic justice in 15 minutes, which is a fairly typical presentation length. If you try, you are unlikely to get as far as even what should be the starting point. This is a difficult point to communicate successfully.

If you choose one case and discuss a limited number of points from that case, you are likely to be able to produce an analytical piece of work. In presentations, the miniature is the ideal. Obviously, your tutors may have provided the topic, or more frequently a list of topics for you to choose from, but even here you should be looking to produce an analytical piece from within the topic rather than a commentary on the topic itself.

So, for example, if the topic you have been given is the right to a fair trial under Article 6 of the European Convention on Human Rights and you look in a textbook for some material, you will find that a fairly basic description of how the Article works in the jurisprudence of the European Court of Human Rights is far beyond the scope of what your presentation could contain. This is because you are looking, as the textbook writer must, at the macro level of the topic. To look at the micro level, typically the single case approach, you will see that the basis of some of the jurisprudence is developed from the case of *Albert and Le Compte v Belgium*. Using this case as the basis for your research will limit your coverage to one particular aspect of the Article but it will enable you to produce a presentation which is sufficiently analytical within the scope of your presentation time.

Similarly, if your presentation topic is parliamentary sovereignty, you will again find a wealth of case law, far too much for a presentation. However, if you base your coverage on one case, for example *R v Secretary of State for Transport, ex parte Factortame Ltd*, this will bring you down to one particular aspect of parliamentary sovereignty and thus a basis for your research. You will then be able to produce an analytical presentation rather than a purely descriptive one.

What this means, of course, is that from one presentation topic there are a large number of possibilities. Although these will overlap, they will not be the same. If students attempt descriptive pieces on the topic they often are the same. Tutors do not want a descriptive piece of work. It is particularly disappointing if, having told students what is needed, what comes back is a rerun of the lecture. Do not do it.

When tutors encourage this approach the response is frequently that the student is worried that they may be penalised for missing out an important aspect of the topic. The answer is that if the tutor wanted the student to give the lecture on the topic, they would say so. They do not; the tutor has done the lecture, the student is doing a presentation.

An alternative approach is the single article approach. For this you identify, or have had identified for you, a single journal article. As has already been said, journal articles go through a rigorous quality control process so those from reputable law journals can normally be relied on to be authoritative. If you are in any doubt about the status of an article, check with your tutor. As with the single case approach, what you need is to be analytical, not descriptive, but that is what journal articles are, anyway, as are cases. So as long as you do not fall into the trap of simply reporting what an author has written, it should be fairly easy to produce a good piece of work.

The poster presentation

A very different kind of presentation is the poster presentation. This is typically a proposal for a research topic, for example for a dissertation, and is assessed either as part of a research module or as contributing to the mark for the dissertation itself. What your tutors are looking for here is: has the student identified what is needed to approach the research project in an appropriate manner?

This is a very different form of presentation, and although it is easy to do it right it is also equally easy to do it spectacularly wrong. Doing it right is about following instructions and, in particular, learning outcomes and **marking criteria**. If you have your own, then use those, but if not, a separate set of outcomes and criteria for poster presentations are supplied in Appendix 1 (p. 196), and Appendix 2 (p. 203), at the back of this book.

In the subsequent chapters the construction of a presentation will be discussed, followed by advice on how to present.

Summary

This chapter has looked at:

- the nature of presentations;
- their division into two particular elements, the oral presentation and its content;
- the integration of authority into a presentation;
- the small scale of a presentation as opposed to an essay;
- the single case approach and how a topic which is too large can be adapted to fit the scale;
- the single article approach;
- the different nature of a poster presentation.

15 Preparing the Presentation

By the end of this chapter you should be able to:

► identify the basic elements of the presentation;
► use research to fill out those elements;
► draw conclusions.

The structure of an oral presentation

You have a presentation topic – you have either chosen one or been given one – and are now ready to begin your preparation. Where do you start? As with the other forms of assessment, the key is structure, so the first thing that needs doing is to look at where you can develop a structure from. Your lecture notes or textbook, or both, will give you the basic information you need to start. What are the most important elements to the topic? What cases have examined these elements and in what context? Having identified which element of the topic you wish to concentrate on, you can then decide which case or journal article will form the basis of your presentation. What is vital here is not to choose blockbuster cases: for example, *Re A (Children)* [2000] EWCA Civ 254, the case of the conjoined twins, is a popular case with students but is impossible as a basis for presentation because it is 81 pages long. One small aspect of it may be possible but the whole thing is not.

Similarly, in choosing a journal article as the basis of your presentation, either choose one of moderate length or be prepared to select elements of the author's argument and discard others. Also, remember what was said in Chapter 4 (p. 31) about journal articles as sources: those referenced in textbooks may be outdated because of the time taken from writing to publication, so you may need to check for more recent articles using the specialist law databases. This does not necessarily mean that older articles are always suspect – an article 25 years old may still have value – it is merely that they need to be treated with caution since some aspects of the topic will have almost certainly changed. If you are alive to those changes, using older articles can be very rewarding – but if you are not, you risk getting it very wrong. It is bad enough marking a written assignment in which the student has missed the target; listening to them doing it is worse.

Identifying basic elements

The next stage is similar to what has been seen before: identifying the skeleton of the piece. If you are using a case report then the skeleton is the points made by the judge or judges in reaching the decision (remembering always that you may need to be selective as you probably do not have the space for all of them). If this is the case, you need to isolate the elements of the argument that you are going to cover. It is the same with a journal article: look at what elements have made up the author's structure. Again, you may need to be selective, taking one thread of the author's work rather than the whole.

Once you have the skeleton, so that you know what particular elements you are looking for, you can begin your research in textbooks and journal articles covering those elements. Remember always that if you try to do it the other way round you may well be wasting time because you will have researched elements you do not need and you may have missed elements you do need.

Your research will then give you the points made by authors on those elements making up your skeleton so they can be fitted round it, always taking care to compare and contrast what the various authors are saying rather than merely listing their views one after another. This gives you your plan; and then you are in a position to start writing. Be prepared to modify your plan as you go along, as your ideas develop from your writing, but make sure you do not abandon it or you may never find your way back.

How do you know if your method is working to produce a good presentation rather than a bad one? The answer is the same as in the previous areas but with a few additional things added. Are you repeating what was said in the lecture on the topic? If you are then you should not be. You should be looking to start where the lecture stopped. A (very) brief introduction is fine, linking to what was said in the lecture but, as was said in respect of other assignment forms, keep it brief at no more than 10 per cent of the materials (less if possible).

Are you reciting case facts? If you are then you should not be. What you are looking for in cases are the reasons for the decision and those are not in the facts but in the reasons the judge or judges gave for their decision. Case facts are rarely necessary: leave them out.

Are you describing the legal position? If you are then you should not be. Remember what was said in Chapter 3 (p. 13) about description versus analysis: you need very little description and a great deal of analysis – *why* not *what*.

Integrating authority

Those are the negative elements. What of the positive ones? As with other forms of assessment, are you integrating your authority? Is the work comparing what one source has said with another, going from authority to authority on the same point? This should be obvious in two ways. Firstly, the written piece itself should read easily, with authors being compared and contrasted. As you have brought the authority explicitly into the body of the work, as described in the previous chapter, you can check this more directly than with some other forms of assessment. Secondly, as with other forms of assessment, you should be keeping a list of your references and you can check that these references are alternating rather than being a list of one author's views followed by a list of another's (see Chapter 6, p. 55).

Are you making sure you are keeping the **learning outcomes** and assessment criteria in view, both literally and metaphorically? There is no point in your having them if you do not use them, and if you do not have them, use the ones given in the Appendix. Keep them in front of you where you can see them and periodically check that you are doing what they require. If you meet the learning outcomes and assessment criteria you will be doing a good piece of work and that will put you well on the way to a good mark.

As you complete the discussion on each element of your answer, are you drawing conclusions from what has been said? As has been said in respect of other assessments, these conclusions do not need necessarily to come down on one side of an argument or the other – if there was a definitive answer then why would you need the discussion? That the thing is still debatable or that there is much to be said for the different arguments is as valid a conclusion as any.

Are you keeping to the thread of your piece of work, coming back to the central question at the conclusion of each element so that it is one comprehensive piece of work rather than a set of unconnected items? Remember that the connection being in your head is worthless; when you do your presentation your audience needs to hear it – so make sure it is explicit. As has been said before, it usually only needs one sentence added at the end of each point to make the connection.

Concluding a presentation

Once you have completed the piece of work you will need an overall conclusion. However, as with other examples this should be short, not more than 5 per cent of the work, because it is pulling together the conclusions you have been making as you have gone along rather than introducing anything new.

If it introduces something new then it is not a conclusion; it is yet another piece of the argument.

If you have to hand in a written version of your work, you now have it. This is useful as normally your tutors need to have material to show the External Examiner and a written version of your work is easier to moderate than a video, which is normally the other option.

This has produced the material for your presentation and meets the 'knowledge and understanding' and the 'cognitive and intellectual' skills parts of the learning outcomes. The next chapter will look at how to turn it into a presentation.

Preparing a poster presentation

For a poster presentation this is the only element since you do not write a complete work or, normally, give a presentation to back up your poster. There may be a face-to-face element with tutors but they will usually be aiming merely to identify if you have understood the task and the elements that have gone into its completion.

The first element is to identify a topic. Practices vary, in that some universities will allow almost complete freedom for the student to choose their own research area whereas others will provide a list of topics from which the student has to choose. Presumably that has been done as part of the earlier work in the research module or dissertation module. What is important at this stage is that it is not too finished an article and can be fairly general because you are going to refine your topic through the completion of the task. The poster presentation is a preparation, not the culmination of it.

Sources for a poster presentation

Once a topic has been identified, the first task is to identify sources as the basis for the research task. Again, your tutors are not at this point looking for a definitive list of all the sources you are going to employ in writing the final work, otherwise you would already have completed half the task, not being at the proposal stage. What they want to know is: can you identify a wide range of sources that are academically authoritative, as the basis for starting your research?

The second element is whether you can distinguish between these sources. Can you show which are primary sources, principally legislation and cases, and which are secondary, mainly textbooks and journal articles, either print or electronic? Most importantly, have you ensured that you have not cited sources that are not authoritative? It is very easy in looking for a wide range of sources to include things such as newspaper articles or websites but since these are not authoritative they will result in your losing marks, not gaining them.

The final element in this part of the task is to select and evaluate relevant information from these sources. If your range of sources is good, this should be fairly simple because the authors you have identified will have taken differing approaches to the topic area and so you can compare and contrast them.

Questions and methodology

Now you have the starting point for the task – your topic and sources – you can identify some of the questions forming the substance of the work you are going to do. Again, these do not need to be the finished article; they are the questions which will give you a starting point for your research, enabling you to look at specific points within the topic rather than approaching it generally.

These questions, and the instructions for your research, will then give rise to the methodology: how are you going to research the topic? For an undergraduate project you are likely to be limited to published sources so methodology is more about identifying further sources which your questions lead you to and building this variety of sources into a structure.

The poster

The key to actually doing the poster on which you are assessed is to keep it simple. What information is required and how has it to be presented? For the answer look at the assessment criteria (if you have not been supplied with your own, see p. 196). If everything on your poster equates to what is required for the top marks, then those are what you will get.

What is *not* needed is a mass of text. This is not the final research task completed, it is how you are going to start it – so limit what is on your poster to the information needed. List your sources, divided into primary and secondary ones and then further divided. This is particularly important with your secondary sources to get a balance between them. You are much more likely to be able to produce a lively and interesting piece of work if you have identified sources (most importantly journal articles) which challenge each other and you have articulated in your questions how they have done this.

After your sources, you can list the questions they have yielded, identifying the sources for each question and demonstrating opposing sides to them and the authors taking those sides. These questions lead to your central question and the methodology.

Note what has not been said: there are no marks for artistic impression. The purpose of the poster is to transmit the information required. If it does so, it will produce good marks; if it does not do so, it will not. It is very easy, especially if you have not done one of these before, to think that something striking will produce better marks. If the pursuit of impact causes you to lose the material on which you are being marked, it will have the opposite effect.

Summary

This chapter has looked at:

- identifying the skeleton of a case or article as the basis for a presentation;
- researching to identify the material to build on this to produce an authoritative and analytical piece of work;
- applying the skills learned earlier in the book to writing the presentation material, alternating views rather than listing them, avoiding repeating lecture notes, case facts and descriptions;
- drawing a conclusion from each point and maintaining the thread of the discussion by bringing the topic back in explicitly each time;
- providing a short conclusion;
- understanding the methodology behind a poster presentation.

16 How to Present

By the end of this chapter you should be able to:

► use visual aids to enliven your presentation;
► appreciate the fine line between too much information and too little;
► understand how to use a script;
► appreciate the value of an introduction;
► understand the difference between what is written and what is said.

Communication

Now that you have written your presentation, the question arises as to what you do with it. The one thing you do *not* do is just take the script with you and read it! Firstly, that would mean your head was buried in the script, giving the audience nothing to look at apart from the top of your head, which is unlikely to be your most expressive feature. Secondly, it removes from the presentation anything that would make it a presentation: that is, something to hold the audience's attention, thus enabling what you are saying to be communicated. Most people have seen presentations or lectures done this way – you probably have, and know how awful it can be. The lesson must be not to do it.

Visual aids

The easiest way to help you to communicate is the use of visual aids. These are your props, something that will, for some of the time, take the attention away from you and concentrate it on the screen, board, chart or whatever else you are using. However, as with anything else, it is not just a question of using visual aids; it is about using them well. Although there are many types of visual aids, the most common is the PowerPoint presentation and that will be used as the basis of what follows. Remember that the lessons apply to all types of visual aids. The rules are the same; it is merely the medium that changes.

Again, it is not just about using a PowerPoint presentation; it is about doing it well. If you have seen presentations that have been done badly because the presenter has not known how to do one, the experience will stick with you. A name has been coined for such presentations, 'PowerPointlessness'. What this generally means is that the presenter has so loaded the visual aids with material that what they say, and indeed their presence, is pointless. It would be as entertaining to give you the slides to read because that is all the presenter is doing.

In order to avoid this you need to tread a fairly fine line between the slides being useless because they are superfluous and their being overloaded with material. What the slides should show is headings and prompts, things you can use to distract attention away from you at various points. The easiest way of demonstrating this is to show an example that was used earlier on the differing opinions in the House of Lords' decision of *Airedale NHS Trust v Bland*. It was said that your script could look something like this:

Sample script

In *Airedale NHS Trust v Bland* the judges in the House of Lords agreed that it would be lawful for doctors to cease the treatment of Tony Bland with the result that he would die. However, the route by which they reached this conclusion differed. Lord Goff considered that the solution lay in the proposition that the right of self-determination should not be lost by virtue of incompetence. This is approaching, but not quite reaching, a substitute decision test: that is, making the decision the judge believes the patient would have made if he had been capable. Lord Browne-Wilkinson, on the other hand, said that the duty to provide treatment to the incompetent patient ended when the treatment ceased to be of benefit to the patient. Moreover, he said that at that point to continue treatment would be unlawful.

The approach that is of little value, because it gives you too little to work with, would be a static slide which added nothing. It might be something like this:

Airedale NHS Trust v Bland

Lord Goff

Lord Browne-Wilkinson

The opposite fault, which is much more common and frequently happens with staff as well as students, is the overloaded slide. This might look like this:

Airedale NHS Trust v Bland

House of Lords

- It would be lawful for doctors to cease the treatment of Tony Bland with the result that he would die.
- The route by which they reached this conclusion differed.
- Lord Goff – the solution lay in the proposition that the right of self-determination should not be lost by virtue of incompetence.

This is approaching, but not quite reaching, a substitute decision test.

- Lord Browne-Wilkinson – the duty to provide treatment to the incompetent patient ended when the treatment ceased to be of benefit to the patient.

At that point to continue treatment would be unlawful.

There are two main problems with this. The first, as was said earlier, is that it renders the script irrelevant and effectively you would just be reading the slides. This is not the most entertaining of experiences for your audience. The second problem is that, in order to get the information on the slide, the print size has to be reduced thus making it hard for your audience to read it.

In order to provide you with a prop, something to assist in your presentation, you need prompts but not the actual script. A suitable slide for this part of your presentation might look something like this:

Airedale NHS Trust v Bland

House of Lords

Ending treatment lawful – Result death

- *Lord Goff*
  Self-determination
  Substitute decision

- *Lord Browne-Wilkinson*
  Duty to treat ceases
  Treatment becomes unlawful

This gives you something that is not cluttered, is easy for the audience to see and that provides you with a distraction for the audience, moving them away, for a few seconds at a time, from looking just at you. If your slides have approximately this much information on each, that is enough. If it looks as though a slide is becoming overloaded, just spread the information over two slides like this:

Airedale NHS Trust v Bland

House of Lords

Ending treatment lawful – Result death

- *Lord Goff*
  Self-determination
  Substitute decision

Airedale NHS Trust v Bland

House of Lords

Ending treatment lawful – Result death

- *Lord Browne-Wilkinson*
  Duty to treat ceases
  Treatment becomes unlawful

If you can, it helps to animate the slide so that each line comes up with a mouse click as you get to that point. So with this slide:

Airedale NHS Trust v Bland

House of Lords

Ending treatment lawful – Result death

- *Lord Goff*
  Self-determination
  Substitute decision

- *Lord Browne-Wilkinson*
  Duty to treat ceases
  Treatment becomes unlawful

if the first two lines come up with the slide, each subsequent line can be clicked up as you get there.

Using a script

So far, this chapter has concentrated on the mechanics of the presentation, but there is one more thing to consider before looking at actually doing it. That is the question of how you are going to deal with your script. As was said earlier, just reading it out is a very audience-unfriendly way of presenting. Students, and others, sometimes try to learn a script by heart but this is very difficult, particularly if you are nervous about doing the presentation. It is easy to forget things, miss things out, get lost and generally do it badly.

The best method here is the use of prompt cards. A useful size is something like 10 cm x 7.5 cm, on which you write the main points of your script including any references, quotes and other key information. Make sure the writing is sufficiently large to enable you to focus on it easily, otherwise you will either be straining to read the cards or bringing them up to mask your face – this is why you need it to be the key points of the script and not the whole thing. Also mark on the cards where the next click is for your PowerPoint slides so that what you are saying will be synchronised with the slides. As you become more practised at presentations you will be able to reduce the amount of material you put on your prompt cards, leaving only quotes and references, but do not try this to begin with as you need to build up both technique and confidence first.

An alternative is to use the 'notes' facility on PowerPoint and print the slides and notes at one slide per page. If you take this approach beware of slipping into the same fault as if you had a complete script. Make sure you have something to place the pages on so you can use them without holding them.

Rehearsing the presentation

You now have the script, slides and prompt cards – so you are ready to practise doing the presentation itself. One common problem at this stage is that students read their presentations silently to themselves and panic because it takes less than half the allocated time. They then add more material. When doing the presentation they then overrun massively, or are stopped by the tutor when the time is up halfway through the material. The reason for this is that when you read silently, you read much faster than is comfortable for an audience. When practising you need to read out loud at a moderate pace. It is best if you can have someone as an audience to help you get the pacing right; alternatively you might record yourself so you can hear how it sounds. When you are practising, ensure that your voice tone varies (there is little more boring than a monotone) and that you pause when an important point is made so that your audience can consider it for a second or two.

Once you are reasonably confident with using your cards you can bring in your PowerPoint. At this stage you can think about further animation – of you, rather than your slides. How are you going to stand, sit, move, and do the things that will keep the audience interested and concentrating on what you are saying? It is better to stand if you can as this makes movement easier but some students need to sit because they are so nervous they cannot stand. Make sure that you are facing the audience and that whatever the mouse and cards are placed on is close by. For this purpose many people like to use a lectern, a reading stand, as it is a useful place for the mouse and cards and enables you to click without moving away. Place yourself to one side of the screen and fairly close to it so that when you turn to the screen you do not have your back to the audience.

In the presentation itself you need to look at the audience, not concentrating on one person all the time but taking in the whole room – so practise this. When a new point comes up on your slide turn towards the screen (if you are properly positioned the audience can still see your face) and gesture at it to take the view of the audience away from you and to the screen for a few seconds before returning to you. This audience eye movement helps concentration and lessens the possibility of someone falling asleep, which is easy to do if you are looking in one place for any length of time. Once you have become sufficiently skilled at this technique you can move the lectern slightly further from the screen and walk from the lectern to the near edge of the screen to point to the material you have just clicked up.

For most presentations there is a requirement to dress formally, as you would if you were working and doing the presentation as part of your job. As you can see from the marking template in Appendix 1 (p. 193), this is something for which you can be marked up or down. A suit is the usual requirement. Even if you are not told you have to dress formally, do it anyway. The reason for this is that it creates a good impression with the audience and, more importantly, it gives you the feeling of its being a formal occasion and so helps with the delivery of the material.

The presentation

Always begin by introducing yourself and your topic:

'Good morning, my name is … and my presentation today is on …'

It helps if this information is also on your first slide as the only material on that slide. Try to be aware of what your hands and feet are doing; nervous students tend to play with their clothing or hair. If you find that you do this, hold the lectern with both hands unless you are gesturing towards your slides or moving to the next card. Feet should both be flat on the floor unless you are moving towards the screen. This avoids the distracting sight of a student standing first on one foot and then on the other, appearing to do a dance throughout the presentation. Ensure that the volume is loud enough for everyone in the room to hear you comfortably without your shouting and, as was said earlier, keep your pace moderate and your intonation sufficiently varied. As you can see, these are also elements on the marking template.

Most importantly, make it look as if you are enjoying the experience – and if you do it well you will find that you will. Do not worry about feeling a little nervous before you start. No matter how long you have been doing performances this is likely to happen and is a good thing. Students tend to think that lecturers, because they have been lecturing for some time, do not have this problem. This is not true; it is just that with experience you learn to hide it better. If you read or hear interviews with professional musicians and actors you will know that the same thing happens to them before every performance. This is your performance. The aim is to ensure that all your marks on the marking template are at the right-hand side and then your presentation mark will be a good one. If you have followed the advice in the earlier chapters about the content of the presentation and matched it with the **learning outcomes** and **marking criteria**, you will score well on that too. The result will be a first-class overall mark – and you will have achieved your aim.

Writing v. saying

There are some important differences between what you write conventionally in a law assignment and what you say, and you need to know what these are. Here are some of the most important ones:

Write	Say	Context
R	The Crown	
v	and	
Examples:		
R v R	The Crown and R	A criminal case
Kennedy LJ	Lord Justice Kennedy	A Court of Appeal judge
Laws J	Mr Justice Laws	A High Court judge

Although people manage these most of the time, there is a problem with the first one. Just so that there is no doubt, to say 'R and R' is wrong. The other item to note here is accuracy, as most people can be reasonably accurate in written work but say inaccurate things in lectures and presentations. One of the most common is referring to the Children Act 1989 as 'the Children's Act'; it is not, so do not do it.

Summary

This chapter has looked at:

- the main points of how to present;
- visual aids and how they should and should not be done;
- the mechanics of presentation;
- the need for variety of pace and intonation and knowing how to stand and move;
- the importance of an introduction, and what to do and not to do whilst giving a presentation;
- accuracy and the differences between the way some things are written in law assignments and how they are said.

Part 5

Moots

17 What Are They?

By the end of this chapter you should be able to:

▶ appreciate the nature of an assessed moot;
▶ follow mooting rules;
▶ understand how moots are assessed.

The mooting problem

If you ask people – and by this we mean those involved in legal education – what a moot is, a large number will reply that a moot is a mock trial. It is not. In a trial you have evidence, witnesses for both parties, examination of witnesses, cross-examination and, if it is a jury trial, a summing up by the judge. In a moot you have none of these.

A moot is a mock staged appeal to the High Court (rarely, as the High Court has a very limited appellate jurisdiction) and to the Court of Appeal or Supreme Court most commonly. This means that, most importantly, the facts found in the (usually imaginary) original trial are fixed and there is no scope for arguing them. This is sometimes difficult to get across to students who want to do just that. Because the facts are fixed, what the two sides are disputing is the law applicable to those facts. The reason for this is that, in general, an appeal from a court of first instance can only be made on the basis of an error of law, a procedural fault or because the court made a finding that no reasonable tribunal could have made. It is not impossible to have a moot based on these last two possibilities but it is rare, so this Part will concentrate on appeals that question what the law is.

There are also two very different types of moot. One is the competitive moot in which teams compete against each other. This might be within an institution in the form of an in-house mooting competition, a competition involving law schools from neighbouring universities, a regional competition, or one of the growing number of national competitions. This Part is not about these because assessment should not involve competitive mooting.

The form of mooting that is to be covered is the assessed moot, one which you do as an assessed part of the course of study for a law degree. Even here there are a number of different forms. The most common form is a moot as part of a Legal Method or Legal Skills course, which is normally undertaken in the first year of an undergraduate law programme. A moot may also appear as an assessment in other subjects on a law degree, in any year, and the subject it appears in makes for very different types of moot, particularly if the law subject is Evidence. Lastly, an increasing number of institutions are establishing Mooting options as final-year subjects. Although what is said in this Part is relevant to all these, it will concentrate on the first: the moot as an assessed part of a general, first-year course.

This has important implications. The most obvious negative implication is that although you will be mooting in teams, normally two students for each side, you are not competing against the other side. The most important positive implication is that despite there being four students in each moot, you will be, or should be, assessed individually. The combined effect of these two facts is that you should not see the opposing students as opponents but as colleagues because it is most likely that your individual mark will benefit from a moot in which the standard is generally high rather than a moot in which you try to stand out as particularly competent in a below-standard performance. This does not mean cheating by breaking the rules but it does mean that you should share as much as you can within the rules to raise the general level.

Mooting rules

The first item you need for your moot is the rules. Without these you can do nothing. So that this part of the book makes sense, some rules are needed. Whatever you do, do not use these for your moot, unless your tutors have told you that these rules are the ones they want you to use. Use the ones you have been set.

Sample mooting rules

1. Each moot shall consist of four participants who will be listed as lead counsel for the **appellant**, junior counsel for the appellant, lead counsel for the **respondent** and junior counsel for the respondent.
2. The mooting case facts and grounds of appeal will be provided at least 2 weeks before the date of the moot.
3. Counsel for the appellant and counsel for the respondent shall be permitted to cite up to four cases each side in addition to the cases listed in the mooting problem.
4. Counsel must provide a bundle of documents to the judge and opposing counsel at least 2 clear working days before the moot.
5. Each bundle must include the list of cases to be cited, statutory material and a skeleton argument from each participant on their designated grounds of appeal.
6. Each skeleton argument must not exceed one side of A4 paper in 12 point Arial font at 1.5 line spacing.

7. The order of speaking will be: lead counsel for the appellant, lead counsel for the respondent, junior counsel for the appellant, junior counsel for the respondent. Each will speak for no more than 10 minutes.
8. No case or statutory material may be cited unless contained in the mooting problem or in either bundle of documents.

What is important about these rules is that they are just that, rules. Do not be tempted to break any of them as you can be failed on an assessed moot for breaking a single rule. Most importantly, do not cite any case which is not contained in the mooting problem, the appellant's cases or the respondent's cases.

You will be given the mooting problem which will contain the facts of the case, the initial decision or the judge's instructions to the jury and the grounds of appeal. Do not attempt to go outside these because any departure will be penalised. Unless specifically permitted by your mooting rules, do not use any academic literature in your moot. Some rules do allow citation from textbooks and journal articles, in which case it is permitted to the extent provided but even then it is inadvisable as, with limited exceptions, it is not normal in real-life appeals for academic sources to be used. The problem will also specify which ground or grounds of appeal are to be covered by each participant. Normally in short-form moots with up to 10 minutes per participant, there will be only one ground of appeal each. Longer forms may have more.

Moot assessment

The remaining items you need are the **learning outcomes** for the moot and the assessment criteria and matrix. If you have these, use them; if they are not provided for you there are sample ones in the Appendices (p. 198, p. 188 and p. 194 respectively). Now you have the material, you can progress to how to use it. This is normally in two parts: the research and skeleton argument, and the moot itself. These two parts are frequently marked separately and the marks then aggregated, so you need to concentrate on what is being looked for in each part. The next two chapters will look at these parts.

Summary

This chapter has examined:

- the general provisions relating to moots as a form of assessment on a law degree;
- a set of sample mooting rules, stressing the importance of not departing from those rules or the facts and grounds of appeal in the mooting problem;
- learning outcomes, assessment matrices and **marking criteria**.

18 Research for a Moot

By the end of this chapter you should be able to:

▶ recognise grounds of appeal;
▶ research cases;
▶ understand the importance of judicial precedent in mooting;
▶ build an argument;
▶ produce a skeleton.

Getting started

Researching for a moot is a much more specialised form of research than that for other forms of assessment. The reason for this is that the materials you research are only those that would be admissible in court. Normally this would exclude textbooks and journal articles but would include not only cases and statutes but also other materials such as Law Commission Reports or government White Papers on which the statutes were based.

One thing you do not have to do is work out what the problem is about. You will be given the grounds of appeal and, once you know which role you are playing, you will know which ground of appeal is yours and whether you are arguing for it or against it. Probably the most important rule to remember here is that you must not go outside the ground of appeal you are given; if you do depart from the given ground of appeal you are likely to fail. Similarly, as was said in Chapter 17, do not dispute the findings of fact made by the judgment or verdict you have been given. Those are fixed and to dispute them can also lead to failing the assessment. This actually makes researching and doing your moot much easier than doing other forms of assessment since what you are doing is much more narrowly focused.

The first thing to determine is: do you know what your ground of appeal means? In the normal, first-year moot the meaning of the grounds of appeal should be something you have covered in the course and so it should be fairly straightforward. If you do not know what the ground of appeal means then use your lecture notes or textbook to find out. Moot problems in later stages can be more complex and may be on areas of law you have not covered, so you will have to learn those areas before continuing.

Cases for the moot

Once you do know what the ground of appeal you are arguing means, you can start your research by reading the case or cases that have been used in the problem. Do not be tempted to try to save yourself time by reading only the headnote. You need to read the judgment in full; and if there is more than one, read them all. You will find that most of what you need for your point of law will be in a fairly small part of the judgment but there will be other parts that are needed. One of these is the summary of the facts of the case, as it may be that there is a sufficient difference between the facts of your case and the one cited to distinguish it – that is, for the opposite decision to be made because of the differences in case facts. When you have identified the part of the judgment which relates to your ground of appeal the first thing to ensure is that you understand the argument. If you have a problem with this, go back to your textbooks or lecture notes to find an explanation.

Once you have understood the point of law you are going to argue and how the judge or judges in the cases cited in the problem have addressed this, you then need to find additional cases in which this point of law has been discussed. You will probably find that some have been cited in the cases you were given with the problem. The question to consider before deciding to use them is whether they help with the point of law you are arguing. Because you need to put forward an argument either opposing the reasons given in the problem (if you are counsel for the **appellant**), or supporting them (if you are counsel for the **respondent**), you need to find cases supporting your view. If there are none of these in the problem and the cases cited do not give you any then you need to find something that will support your case. Here your textbooks can be useful as a source of cases, but do not rely on textbooks for the reasoning: go to the case and read it yourself.

Before you start putting your argument together, remember to use your case-law databases to check for any recent decisions in the area (see p. 77). The easiest way to do this is to use the case relied on in the judgment as your search term. This will produce any recent cases in which the point of law you are arguing has been discussed and so will help you with your point of law. Do not be tempted to miss this stage of the research: it will be detrimental to your moot if there is a recent case on the point and you do not cite it. This is particularly important if it has reached a different conclusion from the case cited in your problem. It is extremely painful for a 'judge' in a moot to hear counsel arguing a point based on a case in which the decision has been reversed on appeal or has been overruled.

Once you have assembled your cases you need to check if there are other materials you need. If the decision in your case was made on the basis of a provision of the common law or **equity**, the answer is likely to be no. However, if the decision revolves around a statutory provision there is at least the Act to consider and possibly any preparatory materials that would give the reasoning behind the provision such as Law Commission Reports or government White Papers. If these do exist you would need the relevant parts of these as well.

Precedent

Once you have assembled your materials the question arises as to what you are going to do with them. Always be aware that you are arguing for a particular interpretation of one individual point of law as it applies to your problem. This has several important repercussions. The most important one is the matter of precedent. If you are arguing a case where the leading authority is a Supreme Court or House of Lords decision, do not argue that that decision is wrong unless the decision dated from before the Human Rights Act 1998 and an interpretation of that Act would change the original decision, or there has been a change brought about by another statute. This applies even if you are, in theory, arguing the case in the Supreme Court, unless you can bring the 1966 Practice Direction into play. This said that precedent is an indispensible foundation and that:

> while treating former decisions of the House of Lords as normally
> binding they would depart from a previous decision when it appears
> right to do so bearing in mind the danger of disturbing settled law
> and especially the need for certainty in the criminal law.

When you have looked at this on your course you will see that this is a very rare event and one on which it is unwise to base your mooting argument.

The result of this is that if your problem is one where there is a binding precedent on the 'court' you are appearing in, the technique is to distinguish that precedent on the basis that the differences in facts between your case and the precedent case mean that the reasoning in the precedent case does not apply to your case. This early in your law course this should not normally happen, there should not be such a strongly binding precedent, but mistakes can be made in setting mooting problems and you need to be aware of what to do if it happens to you.

The more normal mooting position at this stage is that there will be authority but it will not be binding authority. In this case you can argue either or both of the propositions that the authority is wrong or that your case can be distinguished from it. If, from your reading of the cases you have, you can argue both then do; if only one is possible then argue that one.

Building your argument

Now that you know what you are going to do, you need to look at how you are going to do it. You need to construct an argument in favour of your side's interpretation of the point of law and against the other interpretation. If you are counsel for the appellant it is the interpretation which was the basis for the original decision which you need to argue against, and if you are counsel for the respondent it is the point of law in the grounds of appeal that you are arguing against. This is a much simpler process than those required for other assessments but you can use the same sort of technique.

The first element of this is to determine the main points of your argument by identifying from the cases the basis of the decision. These points form the spine of your argument just as the relevant points did for other forms of assessment. This is then built on, not with academic authority as in other forms of assessment but, normally, exclusively with authority drawn from your cases. (The only exception to this is the example noted above where you may have the authority of a Law Commission Report or a government White Paper as additional authority; see Chapter 4, p. 32.) When filling out your spine do remember that the number of cases you can use is restricted to those in the problem you have been given plus the number of additional cases allowed. At this stage do not use any more. You will need to agree with your partner which additional cases you are using, so it is probably better at this stage to use half the number your side is allowed as additional cases until this is done. Any other cases that might help can be kept in reserve for use if there is space in your allowance.

As with other forms of assessment, remember that what you are using is authority, not narrative (see Chapter 3, p. 13). Any case facts you introduce must be used only to distinguish your case from any authority. Otherwise all you are using is argument, pointing out from the authorities where the judges have supported the points you are making and opposing the points of your opponents. Your quotations from the judgments need to be kept as short and pointed as possible, in part so that your argument is easy to follow, in part because of your time limit.

Now that the planning is done, you can write what you are going to say. It is at this point that you need to be extremely careful, as with the time normally permitted for assessed moots your scope is very limited. For a 10-minute moot, around 1000 words is probably the maximum, and for a 15-minute one, 1500 words. If you try to say more than this you will either be timed out – the judges will stop you when you reach the time limit – or you will have to speak so fast it will be unintelligible. Both would be grounds for a poor mark and may lead to failing. It is better to be slightly under the time limit than run the risk of being over it.

Once you and your partner have written your arguments you can get together and check what each has done so that you are not overlapping into each other's point of law. Check also your additional cases, to make sure you have not gone over the limit and to decide whether you have space for any further additional cases. If you do have additional space you need to decide between you which of your reserve cases you wish to use and to what purpose. You can then redraft your argument slightly to include the additional authority.

Skeleton arguments

You are now in a position to draft your skeleton argument and list of cases. You already have these: the skeleton argument is the spine you used initially and the cases you used to fill it out, without the quotes from the cases which you used for your full speech. Again, be very conscious of word or space limits for your skeleton argument because any breach will lead to a poor mark and possibly failing. Normal limits would be about one side of A4 paper (as in the sample rules in Chapter 17) or 300–400 words. Your skeleton argument and list of cases can now be submitted to the judges and your opponents.

When you have the skeleton arguments of your opponents you need to check that you have anticipated their points correctly. If both you and the person you are arguing against have used the problem correctly then you will have; if there are points you did not cover, check if you need to cover them. If your opponent has gone outside the grounds of appeal, do not be tempted to follow; but if there is a point that is within the grounds of appeal which you had not anticipated, be prepared to amend your case accordingly. If it is necessary at all it should be a small amendment – but remember, if you add something you will need to cut something out to stay within your time limit.

You are now ready to start practising what you are going to say, but first you will need to consider the ways in which you do this. These are covered in Chapter 19.

Summary

This chapter has discussed:

- restricting research for a moot to case law, statutes and preparatory materials;
- keeping to the grounds of appeal given with the problem;
- using the grounds of appeal and cases cited in the problem;
- researching these and other cases to support your argument;
- constructing a spine from these materials to form a logical argument and filling it out with supporting materials;
- using the spine and the cases in it as your skeleton argument to submit to the judges and your opposition;
- checking the skeleton argument from your opposition to ensure you have covered all their points.

19 Presenting a Moot

By the end of this chapter
you should be able to:

▶ appreciate why formal
dress is important;
▶ address judges
correctly;
▶ adopt appropriate body
language and voice
pitch;
▶ perform a moot.

Dress

The general rules on presentation were covered in
Chapter 16 (pp. 131–8), but presenting a moot is a
specialised form and so you need to prepare carefully.
What you are doing is mimicking what a barrister
would do in an appeal but on a much smaller scale. As a result, the things
you do must be what would be done in court.

The first item to consider is dress. If your rules state that a particular form
of dress be worn, then that is what you must do. Some institutions require
that gowns be worn and if they do, they should provide them. In general,
rules are either silent on this aspect or just specify gowns. In either case the
clothes you wear should be formal and this means a dark suit, white shirt
and sober tie for men, and a dark suit, with either trousers or a skirt, and a
white blouse for women. There are several reasons for this. The first is that if
you are going to act the part it helps to look it, and formal dress places you
in the context of the occasion. Casual clothing implies an informal situation
and this is not the impression you are trying to make. In addition, a gown
over casual clothing is a mess. You may have noticed that the **marking
criteria** for moots in the Appendix (p. 194) even include a section on dress
and although you are unlikely to be marked down by much on that aspect
alone, the air of formality given by the appropriate clothing does feed over
into other parts of the marking criteria. As this book is about getting good
marks, you need to do all that you can in pursuit of them.

Modes of address

Just as with dress, the way you address the judge or judges is an important
part of the performance. Individual judges should always be referred to as
'my Lord' or 'my Lady' as appropriate. If you are referring to judges as a
bench, an all-male or mixed bench of judges should be referred to as 'my
Lords', an all-female bench as 'my Ladies'. If a judge has intervened to ask

you about a particular point, that judge should be replied to as 'your Lordship' or 'your Ladyship' as appropriate. That said, it is important that you do not exaggerate the use of these titles. You opening should start with the relevant form and your final sentence should also include it, but in between restrict use to where you are seeking to emphasise a point. There is little that sounds as false as every sentence beginning with titles, yet it can be tempting when you are nervous.

As with the judges, your colleague and your opponents should be referred to formally as 'my learned friend'. If it is necessary to distinguish between others taking part in the moot you should refer to 'my learned friend' and then their title (Mr, Mrs, Miss or Ms) and their surname. It is even more important in this context that you do not overdo such references and it may be that you could get by without using them at all; however, this is not a good idea as one of the things that will be being assessed is mode of address (see p. 195), and so you need to use the form, if only once, to show that you can do it.

Body language

When you are speaking, face the judges directly unless you are referring to your colleague or an opponent, in which case you turn briefly to them before returning to face the judges. This is important as little undermines an argument more than an avoidance of eye contact and, as you can see from the moot marking criteria provided, this is one of the elements of the marking. It is easier if there is more than one judge as you can change focus from time to time and, obviously, if a judge has intervened to ask you something then you should address that judge directly with your reply.

You will also notice a reference to body language. What this means is that you should be standing straight, head up and using your hands to emphasise points in your argument. Make sure you do not put your hands in your pockets or use them to play with your clothing or hair. This is very easily done if you are nervous but it gives a bad impression. The best way to avoid the temptation is to hold whatever you are using for your argument rather than placing it on a lectern or desk. Do not wander about; there should be minimal foot movement, and make sure you are standing with both feet firmly on the floor. This will avoid the problem frequently seen when inexperienced students are performing in a moot – that of the student standing predominantly on one foot and moving the other nervously. Again, this is a distraction and should be avoided.

Voice

The most important elements, however, relate to your voice and your argument. The argument has been covered in Chapter 18 – but what do you need to do with your voice? The first thing you need is to be thoroughly prepared and, as the position here is the same as for presentations, see what was said in Chapter 16 (p. 135) about the use of cards rather than a script and the importance of practising your speech. You will see that the sections relating to Speech on the mark sheet are divided into volume, intonation and pace. When someone is nervous, what tends to happen is that they either speak too quietly or they shout; they might speak in a high monotone and far too fast.

First, look at volume. This will depend very much on the venue you are doing your moot in. If you are in a small room such as a seminar room you will be able to speak in a normal conversational tone and everyone in the room will be able to hear you. If you are in a larger room then you will need to project your voice more. If you have lecturers who can be heard at the back of a lecture theatre without using a microphone or shouting, study how they do it. The trick is about voice projection rather than volume; and if you practise in a room the size of the one you are going to use with a friend sitting at the back, you should be able to master the technique.

The next factor is intonation. As nervousness tends to lead to a higher voice pitch, it is useful if you practise your moot using the lower part of your normal tonal range. When you are speaking normally the voice changes pitch as you are speaking so you need to ensure this happens with your speech too. If you can, record yourself practising; if not, get whoever is listening to you – and this could be your partner on the moot – to tell you if you are varying your tone enough. If you practise this thoroughly it will come to you naturally when doing the moot itself.

The third element is pace. Again, being nervous makes you want to speed up but it is important that, in combating that tendency, you do not slow down too much. This is why it was said in Chapter 18 that you must stick to strict limits on the length of your speech. If you make it too long then you will rush to get through it and so speak too fast to be understood. Remember that you are trying to persuade someone of your argument and you will not do that if they are unable to follow it. If it turns out that you have miscalculated and look as though you are going to overrun, cut a piece of what you were going to say rather than gabble or run the risk of going over time and being stopped before you have reached your conclusion.

● **Performing**

The first thing you must do, if you are the leader for your side, is to introduce yourself and your colleague properly. You will see this is referred to in the marking criteria in the Appendix. To do this when a judge asks who is appearing for the **appellant** or **respondent**, you stand up (never address the judges from a sitting position), and say your name and the name of your colleague with their title.

You also have some props which you need to use correctly: these are your skeleton argument and your authorities, both of which you have provided to the judges. As your skeleton argument is the skeleton of your speech, refer to it along the lines of:

'As you will see, my Lords, in the skeleton argument ...'

and when referring to the cases or other authority link it with your list of authorities and skeleton argument:

'As was stated in the skeleton argument on the authority of *X v Y* at paragraph 56 ...'

If the judges have the law reports in front of them (as they normally do in competition moots), make sure you stop and ask if they have the reference, and only start quoting it when they do. This is less likely in assessed moots but much will depend on the format your lecturers have chosen. As long as you know how to do it, you will not have a problem. Using your authorities like this is what is covered by items 8 to 11 in the Assessment Criteria for Moots in the Appendix, and these are the technical aspects of mooting which differ from any other form of assessment. If you get these right you will improve your marks drastically, which is what you are aiming to do.

One thing which students often have difficulty with in mooting is judicial intervention. Because they have a script, they want to follow it and are inclined to respond unhelpfully to judicial interventions. It should be that in a first-year assessed moot there will be little or no judicial intervention (things change later), but if the judges do intervene you need to be prepared to deal with it.

The first thing to remember is that in intervening in an assessed moot the judges are not trying to catch you out; they are trying to help you. This is often the case in competition moots as well, and judicial intervention is an attempt to steer you in a particular direction or to add clarity to something you have said or perhaps omitted to say. The one thing you must not do is ignore the intervention. If you can reply briefly to what the judge has asked, then do so; the judges should allow extra time for judicial intervention and its response. If you cannot respond, then say why. It may be that the question is outside the scope of your ground of appeal, so say that it is and, if it is within your colleague's ground of appeal, state that it is something 'to be covered by my learned friend'. There is also nothing wrong with replying to a question by saying that you do not know the answer – you cannot be expected to be an expert on the subject in a year 1 moot.

The last thing you need to do in your moot is to conclude correctly. Just as with any other form of assessment, you need to sum up your argument briefly using around 5 per cent of your word count and time. Be aware that in a 10-minute speech that is only 30 seconds – so do not ramble. You then need a formal concluding sentence such as:

'In view of this, my Lords, I invite you to uphold [or dismiss] this appeal.'

Summary

With cross-referencing to Chapter 16, 'How to Present', this chapter concentrates on:

- the things that are different about presenting a moot;
- the importance of dress;
- forms of address for the judges and colleagues;
- body language and speech, in particular the importance of volume, pace and tone;
- the technical aspects of the use of the skeleton argument and authorities;
- the problem of judicial intervention and how to deal with it;
- the importance of a conclusion and asking the judges to uphold (or dismiss) the appeal.

Part 6

Exams

20 Exam Preparation

By the end of this chapter
you should be able to:

▶ appreciate the need to
prepare for exams;
▶ understand the impor-
tance of practising
exam answers;
▶ know how to revise
and how not to revise.

Why exams?

As was said in Chapter 1, students often approach staff
quite late on in their degree programme, frequently just
before final exams, and say that they 'need' an Upper
Second degree. They are then asked what they have done to ensure this and
the answer is 'nothing'! It can never be stated too often that what you get
out of your degree will reflect what you put into it, and this is particularly so
in respect of exams. Why is this? The answer is that exams are a highly artificial form of assessment. It will be rare in real life that you have to work just
with what you can remember on a problem you have not seen before and
come up with a convincing answer in a very restricted timeframe. Yet this is
what exams do. So why do we have them? Partly it is tradition. In the past
assessments were examinations because requiring people to produce
answers in a designated space and time meant that the examiners could be
sure the candidates had produced the answers and not got them from elsewhere. Some academics are now re-emphasising this because of the availability of bought assignments.

The second answer is much to do with the conservatism of professions
and particularly solicitors and barristers. When the professions had much
more control over Qualifying Law Degrees, the place of assessments other
than exams was strictly limited in the Foundation subjects. Even though that
control has lessened significantly, the professions still push the unseen exam
above other assessment forms.

This chapter is entitled 'Exam Preparation' because unless you prepare
for exams you are unlikely to do well in them. So when do you start? The
answer is: the start of your course or, if your course has already started,
now. Do not think that because the exams are 7 or 8 months away that you
do not need to do anything about them until then. By that time you will have
had all your other assessments taking up your time and you will be hurrying
to do exam revision and therefore will not have the time to do your exam
preparation.

Why prepare? This has much to do with what was said about exams being highly artificial – passing exams well comes naturally to very few people. It is a skill much like any other skill and so it can be learned. Trying to go into an exam without ever having practised the skill is a little like entering the Tour de France without learning first how to ride a bicycle: you might succeed in the end but you will be far behind everyone else, will have fallen off a few times and be suffering from numerous bumps and bruises.

Practising for exams

So how do you practise? The answer is surprisingly easy. When you are doing your course you will have seminars to back up your lecture programme. For these seminars you will have various questions to prepare, initially mostly from lecture notes and textbooks, but as you progress increasingly from journal articles and primary sources such as cases. These seminar questions are normally former exam questions or questions resembling them. In preparing for your seminar, you will look at the question and try to structure and answer it as if it were a miniature assignment. Obviously you will not write it up as an assignment before the seminar takes place but will have it as a set of notes. During the seminar see how your answer matches up with the one arrived at and make sure that you have noted down, in particular, where the eventual answer has differed from yours. Especially important is any element you missed completely. This is the material for your exam practice.

Once you have examined this material and understood where you missed out and why, it will be used as a practice answer. Set the time you will have available for an exam answer in that subject; it should be easy to find as past exam papers tend to be available in libraries and on **VLE**s. Take the question on its own, without the materials from the seminar, and plan an answer in the form in which it was done in the seminar. It is well worth taking up to 20 per cent of your answer time making this plan since a planned answer is much better than one which tumbles out with no structure at all. The planning process is the same as for essays and problem questions, as covered in Chapter 9 (p. 80) and Chapter 12 (p. 103) respectively. Once you have planned the answer, write it as though in an exam in the rest of the time available.

Why has this method of preparation been suggested? The answer is that by doing this a limited number of times (it is not suggested you do this with every seminar question but perhaps with one question every 2 weeks), you will develop the technique of answering questions in a limited time without accessing material other than that in your head. You will have learned to ride the bicycle and so you will be able to reach the finish – in your case the end of your exam – without falling off and unbruised.

For many people this might be enough as it will certainly prepare you for your exams, but there is one further step which may be possible. Ask your tutor if they would look at your answer and mark it; you will be surprised how many will say yes as long as they are not inundated with them (which is another reason for not doing too many). If the tutor agrees and returns your answer, see what the comments are – as was said in Part 1 the mark is the least important thing – and see if you can learn from them what you need to do differently. Then incorporate this in your next effort.

Revising

Assuming that you have had the exam practice, the next part is revising for the exam. What many students try to do is to learn their lecture notes. This is not a good thing to do for two principal reasons. The first is that none of your exam questions are going to ask you to reproduce your lecture notes, yet if all you do is learn them that will be what you will tend to do. (It appears to make little difference telling students not to do this – they do it anyway – but if you avoid this you are unlikely to fall into the trap.) The second reason is that your lecture notes will be fairly heavy with case facts and the one thing you must not do in the exam is recite case facts. What is important is *why* a decision was reached in a particular case, not *what* the facts were. If you do not learn loads of case facts you will not be tempted to reproduce them.

If those are the things you should not do, what should you do? The positives come from what was said earlier in the chapter about using seminar questions which are former exam questions or similar as exam practice. You can now use the stock of seminar materials you have from the seminar series as your learning materials for exam revision. This is why it is vital that you have attended your seminars and taken an active part in them. If you have missed the odd lecture that is not a disaster because you can get the relevant material from a textbook, although it is not something to make a habit of as going to the lecture and participating is less work than trying to learn the material on your own. But having a full set of seminar notes, and having filed them so you can find them when it comes to exam revision time, is invaluable because you have it; it is material you created so you should be able to come back to it and understand it easily and it is in the correct format for your exams.

What is also important in using this material for exam revision is not that you learn it parrot fashion but that you learn why the answer came out as it did, the authorities and principles and how the answer is structured. This will enable you to do the same with the real exam questions you come up against. Note whilst you are doing this how few cases are actually required to answer a question. If you look at your lecture notes you may find that the lecturer has cited several hundred cases, 300 to 350 is fairly common over the course of a lecture programme. What you are likely to use in each exam answer is probably somewhere between six and ten. By learning from your seminar materials, it will be these cases that you will learn about, retain and be able to use in your exam answers.

For many exams that will be sufficient, but for some exams there are additional things you can do. The first type of exam to look at is probably the easiest and that is the seen exam. This is an exam for which you get the question paper, or part of it, in advance and so if there is a choice of questions you can choose which to do in advance and, in all circumstances, you can plan answers. But – and this is a big 'but' – do just that: plan your answer and learn the structure of the answer. What you should not do is write a full answer and try to learn the whole thing, because you will not be able to do it and what you produce in the exam room will be the half-remembered answer, which is unlikely to do you much good. The way you should plan your answer is as if you were doing it for an essay or problem question and so you need to refer back to those chapters, Chapter 10 (p. 84) and Chapter 12 (p. 105), respectively.

A slightly different type of exam is one in which either you are told what the topics of the questions are but not given the actual questions, or the scope of the examination will just be a part of the subject syllabus, possibly because the other parts have been assessed already. In these circumstances you need to be careful about what you do. What you must not do is only learn the number of topics that equals the number of answers you must do. Students who make that mistake frequently find that one of the questions is in a form they are unable to tackle or even that they cannot work out which question is the one on the topic they have learned. To avoid this problem you need to make sure that you have covered about 50 per cent more than you need, so if you have to answer two questions make sure you revise enough for three. That way you have a safety net. If the scope of the exam is restricted then obviously you just revise within the restricted scope. However, again, do not reduce the scope still further in the hope that what you cover will be enough. If it turns out not to be, your result will suffer and much good work will have been wasted.

A further type of exam you may come across is one based on a case study, a scenario you are given in advance without the questions, which you will only get in the exam room. This does not mean you cannot do anything; in fact it means the exact opposite. What the case study has done is narrow the scope of the examination, as the questions will be based on the scenario. As a result you can examine the case study, decide what areas of the syllabus the scenario relates to and revise those areas rather than everything. As the case study is based on what you have already done, you can go through your seminar materials and weed out those clearly not covered, and revise using the rest. This is another method of restricting the scope of an exam.

There are other types of exam – multiple choice, structured exams and so on – but the preparation techniques for these are the same as for those already covered so they need not be done separately.

Summary

This chapter has looked at the importance of preparing for examinations by:

- practising exams in advance;
- doing this using seminar materials;
- getting feedback on your attempts;
- revising not by learning lecture notes but by using seminar materials as revision materials;
- restricting revision not by topic but by what is realistically going to be used;
- using specific techniques for seen exams, exams restricted by topic or exams based on case studies.

21 Sitting the Exam

● Coping with panic

You have an exam. You have revised for it thoroughly
and you go to the venue feeling confident, if a little
nervous. You enter the exam room and find your
place, sit down and arrange pens and anything else you have with you. The
starting time arrives and the invigilator says you can now read the question
paper. You read through the question paper, put it back on the desk and
consider that this question paper is written in Icelandic. You think, 'I do not
speak Icelandic so I cannot do this exam.' Did you think that this only
happens to you?

As was said in the previous chapter, examinations are highly artificial
things and this reaction to them is perfectly normal. What matters is what
you do about it. Do not start writing furiously something that might be relevant because you have learned it – in fact, do not start writing at all. Put the
paper on the desk and ignore it. Sit back in your chair, breathe deeply and let
your pulse return to somewhere near normal from the rate it has rocketed to.
When you have done this – and it may take 5 minutes or so but do not worry,
you have plenty of time – pick up the question paper again and you will
recognise that it is written in English. Find one question (do not worry about
any others for the moment) that means something to you, read it carefully
and start making a plan of how to answer it. Once you have your plan – we
come back to that below – start writing your answer. When you are writing,
other elements of the answer will probably occur to you and if they do,
amend your plan accordingly and then go back to writing your answer. Fairly
early in this process you will find that what you learned during the course of
the year and in your revision has come back to you and you can then carry
on to complete the exam.

To do this, select one question at a time if you have a choice of questions.
Even if you do not have a choice or the choice is constrained by some
means, select your own order of answering questions, starting off with the
ones you are more confident about, leaving those you are less confident
about until later. When you get to the later ones you will probably find that

having built up a head of steam with the earlier questions, the later ones are easier than you envisaged.

What is vitally important is that you follow the instructions you are given on the exam paper. If it says do four questions, ensure that you do four questions. If it says do no more than two questions from Part A, make sure you do no more than two questions from Part A. Why do you have to follow the instructions? It is quite simple: any answers you do in breach of the instructions will not be marked and so your grade will suffer. If you want a good grade, and this is what this book is about, then follow the instructions.

How exam marking works

One problem which arises frequently is that students instructed to do four questions only do three and students instructed to do three questions do two. They then wonder why they get poor marks. This arises from a misunderstanding of the marking process.

The way this works is that each question is marked separately, normally out of 100. When your tutors are marking the exams they will normally mark all question 1 first, then all question 2 and so on. Sometimes different tutors will mark different questions on the same exam paper; if you are asked to use separate answer books for separate parts of the exam paper this is normally what is happening. Once all the questions have been marked, the marks will be added up and divided by the number of questions you were instructed to do, not the number you actually did. As a result, if you have only done two questions and you were asked to do three, you have thrown away a third of the marks available. Assuming the pass mark is 40, which is normal for undergraduate programmes, the student who does two questions then must get an average of 60 for those two questions to get 40 overall:

The calculation is $60 + 60 + 0$. Divided by 3 that is $120/3 = 40$

That is just to get a pass mark. To get a good mark is even harder, since to get an overall mark of 60, which should be considered the minimum for a good grade, the student doing only two answers instead of three would need a mark averaging 90 for each of the questions answered.

The calculation is $90 + 90 + 0$ divided by 3 that is $180/3 = 60$

How often are you going to get a mark of 90? Some students think that if they do a really good answer, they will get extra credit which will somehow translate into marks in the absence of one complete question. It will not.

They may get a better mark for that particular question but it will be insufficient to compensate for a missing answer.

Timing the exam

The lesson from all this is that you need to set yourself a timetable for doing the exam and then stick to it. If you are given reading time at the start of an exam, that time should be enough for the de-stressing routine prescribed at the beginning of the chapter. If you do not have reading time, deduct 5 to 10 minutes from the overall time available for the exam. So how much time should you devote to each answer? This is quite easy: apportion your time according to the marks available for each question or part of a question. In standard unseen exams where you are asked to do three or four questions, the normal position is that all questions carry equal marks. As a result you merely divide the time available by the number of questions and that gives the time per question, so a 2-hour exam with reading time and three questions will give a time per question of:

2 hours is 120 minutes so 120 divided by 3 = 40 minutes per question

Similarly, if you have a 3-hour exam and four questions but no reading time, deduct 10 minutes for de-stressing and do the same calculation:

3 hours less 10 minutes is 170 minutes divided by 4 = 42.5 minutes per question

In structured exams – these are exams in different parts with (frequently) different instructions – you do the same thing. So, for example, if a 2-hour exam has three parts and the marks are divided 30:30:40 then the time should be divided in the same proportions. Again, assuming you have reading time this would give:

30 marks times 120 minutes divided by 100 marks = 36 minutes

for parts A and B and:

40 marks times 120 minutes divided by 100 marks = 48 minutes

for Part C. Obviously, you can work out these timings before the exam as you will know what the structure of the paper is going to be.

The important point about these timings is that you stick to them. Do not think that because an answer is going well you should keep going and reduce the time available for a later answer. When you reach the time limit, stop and go on to the next question because, as has been shown, the extra marks will not make up for a missing or half-answered question. That means that 2 or 3 minutes from the time you are due to end a question you should be beginning your conclusion. If you neglect your timings you will not achieve a good grade and much of the work you have put in over the year will be wasted.

Planning

At the start of this chapter reference was made to planning an answer. This is as important in an exam as it is when writing an essay or problem question as an assignment. As a rough guide, it is worth spending between 10 and 20 per cent of your answer time on your plan: that is between 4 and 8 minutes for a 40-minute answer and it should be towards the higher of these figures. So why is this important? The answer is the same as before: your tutors are not looking for you to reproduce your notes or to ramble on generally about a specific area; they are asking you to answer the question set. If you do not plan an answer you are unlikely to do this well and so will not achieve the marks you are aiming for. Obviously, in the constrained situation that is an exam, the planning process is slightly different but it has the same aim: when you reach the end have you answered the question which was set?

Students often believe that there is no time to plan an answer because they have to spend the whole of the examination time writing. This is wrong. Tutors give good marks for well thought-out, well-structured answers which do what the question asks of them. They do not give marks for volume. An answer of 600 to 800 words which does what the question asks will earn many more marks than one which is twice as long and does not. The planning pays off in marks and that is what you are aiming for.

Before starting to plan an answer, you need to consider the mechanics of doing it. It is common for students to plan an answer on the left-hand page of an answer book and then start writing the answer on the right-hand page. This is fine when you are doing the first page of your answer but once you turn the page you no longer have the plan in front of you and it is too easy to deviate from what you intended, in the heat of the exam situation, and so lose the benefit you got from doing a plan originally. The ideal solution is to do your plans in one answer book and your answers in another. If you are given two answer books, and you should be, then this is easy. If you are not, ask for another one for your plans. This way you can keep your plan in front of you and make sure you are following it. If something comes to you part of the way through the answer, do not just follow that idea, amend your plan to include the new item and keep following it.

Using materials in an exam

You may be provided with statutory materials in the exam or you may be allowed to take a statute book in with you. If this is the case, you will get no marks for writing out any of this material in your answer, so do not do it. The material is there for you to refer to if you need to, but if you are prepared as well as you should be, you will not need it. Put it on the floor by the side of your desk and only pick it up if you decide there is something there that you need to check on. You will know how successful your work during the year and your revision have been if you reach the end of the exam without having picked it up.

Planning an essay

If you are answering an essay question, the planning process is the same as that for writing an essay as an assignment in Chapters 7, 9 and 10, modified for the exam situation. First, you decode the question as you were shown in Chapter 7 (p. 72). The decoding process is exactly the same: what is the question asking me, and what are the key words I need to make sure are repeated through the answer?

The planning process is slightly different because you will not have the opportunity to research the answer beyond the knowledge you already have. For first-year exams this will be the lecture and seminar materials which you have used for your revision. Just as with doing an essay as an assignment, you need to begin by defining the terms of the question but, again, keep the factual area short and keep case facts out. The main body of your essay needs to be analytical not factual, as before, and you follow the same rules of authority and not telling stories. You plan your essay skeleton as in Chapter 10 (pp. 85–6), filling it out with authority as you did there and making sure that in your answer the key words run through it. It is unnecessary to give the detail here as you can refer back to the earlier chapters. Although first-year exams can be done with just the lecture and seminar materials this should not be true throughout your course. By your final year your tutors will expect exam answers that go beyond the lecture and seminar materials to materials you have researched yourself. It is common, if this is required, for tutors to tell you the exam topics in advance, so you can choose which areas to research further.

Planning a problem question

As you were shown in Chapter 12 (p. 103) earlier, answering problem questions is easier than answering essay ones because you do not need the decoding stage; the problem decodes the question for you. As a result, answering a problem question in an exam is also easier, because you follow the same process. Students frequently tell tutors that they prefer to answer problem questions in exams rather than essay questions because they are better at them. In fact, this is rarely the case. What they mean is that they find it easy to write problem answers, but in many instances what they write is wrong. They fill answers with case facts rather than just using the cases as authority; they write large chunks of the question when this is completely unnecessary; and rarely do what they are supposed to be doing. What the student perceives as 'being better at the problem question' is actually being able to write large amounts without thinking very much. As with essay questions, in a problem question you will not be awarded marks for volume; you will be awarded marks for applying the relevant areas of law to the facts of the problem, with authority, and drawing the appropriate conclusions.

What you should be doing in answering problem questions in exams is the same as doing them as assignments but the material comes from what is in your head, not your research, and the answers will be shorter, probably 800 to 1000 words rather than the 1500 to 2000 common in in-course assessments.

Conclusions

Whether you are doing an essay question or a problem question, do not forget the importance of a conclusion. This should not be very long, 50 words maximum, but it rounds off an answer and leaves a good impression on the marker with the result that you will get a few more marks for your work.

If you follow these very simple rules, you will do well in your exams. The most important thing is that you come out of the exam knowing that you have done well and can go on to the next one with confidence. Doing something well builds confidence, just as doing something badly destroys it. If you are doing well, you will enjoy what you are doing and so do it better. It always raises a laugh when tutors tell students that the most important thing in the exam is to have fun. But do.

Summary

In this chapter we have shown that:

- panic is normal;
- a de-stressing routine at the start of an exam is a good idea;
- the planning process is in-built;
- answers should be timed to ensure that the paper is completed;
- the marking process is easy to understand;
- the planning and answering routines are slightly modified versions of those in Parts 2 and 3;
- a conclusion is important;
- confidence is built by following these simple rules, which in turn improves results.

Part 7

Dissertations and Extended Essays

22 Identification

By the end of this chapter you should be able to:

▶ appreciate the nature of dissertations and extended essays;
▶ understand the place of a dissertation topic;
▶ identify the learning element in completing an extended work.

What are they?

Dissertations and extended essays look like longer versions of the sorts of assignment you have become used to. An extended essay can be 5000 words or more and undergraduate dissertations 10,000 to 15,000 words typically. They also have another unusual feature, which is that you generally have some choice in the topic. This might be that you choose from a list or that you are given free choice subject to tutor approval. The combination of these two factors can be very good or very bad depending on the way they are approached, and so there are a number of things that need to be considered carefully.

Firstly, writing a 12,000-word dissertation does not mean writing six connected 2000-word essays. If your proposal looks as though this is what you are doing, your supervisor should correct you and send you off to plan a better approach. Not all supervisors do so, and some students do not do what they are told, so they only find out the error when the marks are produced – which is too late. You need to avoid the problem in the first place. The main difference is that in an assignment essay of between 1500 and 2500 words there is a question to be answered. In an extended essay or dissertation there is a topic to be explored or a hypothesis to be tested. In an assignment you start with the question; in a dissertation the title may well be the last thing you write.

Secondly, because you are able to choose what to do, that gives you control of the enterprise and also brings with it the responsibility for the outcome. Tutors try to guide students into areas where there is a great deal of material and real controversy over the area of law. Despite this, students frequently say that they want to do a dissertation on a particular topic; however, when asked what it is about the topic they wish to research, they generally do not know. If a student tells a tutor that they want to do a dissertation on the death penalty, prostitution, abortion or double jeopardy, the tutor's heart sinks because the student clearly has no idea what they are supposed to be doing. Those may be suitable topics for other subject areas but they are not for law. The reason for this is that the law in these areas is clear (in double jeopardy since it was amended in 2003), and the resulting dissertation is likely to be totally descriptive – the type of dissertation which will gain a low lower second-class mark at best and a third or fail at worst. In a dissertation or extended essay the good student should be aiming for a first-class mark because these are easier to achieve in this sort of assessment than in any other. The way to earn a First is to choose an area in which there is much discussion and debate because of serious uncertainties in the law as it stands.

Dissertation topics

In order to identify a suitable topic for the dissertation it is important to bear in mind that this is something that you will be working on for several months. It is not unusual for students to approach tutors in January or February to say that they want to change their dissertation topic because they no longer like it or it has turned out not to be suitable. As the dissertation will have been started in October and is to be submitted in April or May, the student has lost half the time available. It is also the case that in the final year coursework tends to be concentrated in the second term, so time will be even more precious. The chances of combining a dissertation and several assignments in 2 or 3 months instead of 7 or 8 months and achieving good results are small. This problem can be avoided by taking care over your choice of topic in the first place.

It may be that in your second year you have a course on legal research which is geared towards a dissertation topic. If you do, this is a bonus because it enables you to explore possible areas early on. Even if you do not have such a course, it is a good idea to have some idea of a topic by the end of your second year since that will enable you to spend some time over the summer on it and give you a head start for your final year. It may be that you have come across a topic that interests you in the course of your studies, or you may have nothing firm in mind but like a particular area of law that you have studied – or are about to – and believe it will provide you with a dissertation topic. The most important thing to do at this point is talk to your tutor for that subject about it. The tutor will know if it is a suitable topic for an undergraduate dissertation and will be flattered by your interest in their area. The most common reaction of a tutor to a topic is that it is a suitable area for a dissertation but that it is far too wide: a common piece of advice to a student is to choose a topic, halve it, then halve it again, then bring it to us and we will halve it again! The topic the student chose may have been suitable for a book or a PhD thesis but not an undergraduate dissertation.

If you have no idea of a topic, how can you identify one that will provide you with the opportunity for a good dissertation? The most important thing about a dissertation topic is that there is an appreciable amount of academic debate about it so that you have plenty of source material available. It is particularly useful if there are opposing camps in the debate as they will be writing in response to each other endlessly. A good example is the Tony Bland case in 1992 (*Airedale NHS Trust v Bland* [1993] 2 WLR 316), which is still producing journal articles and has done ever since it was decided. It is also worth looking at Law Commission papers over recent years (www.lawcom.gov.uk) to see if there is anything that appeals to you. If you still have no idea, go and talk to your tutors: they may be able to identify something you would like by talking to you.

● The formative element

What is important is merely that you identify a topic area, not the final dissertation. As with all the pieces of work you do on your course, it is important that the dissertation has a formative element – that you learn from doing it – as well as the summative one – that it produces a mark. If you know what you are going to write as your dissertation before you have even started, you are denying it that element and likely to be costing yourself marks. Your tutors will need some indication of the area and what part of it you are considering in order to appoint a supervisor who will be able to guide you, but that is very different from specifying a title before work has started.

Sometimes with dissertations, and most of the time with extended essays, rather than having an open choice students are asked to choose a title from a list. This has the advantage that your tutors will not give you any topics that are unsuitable, such as the ones discussed above; but it has the disadvantage that you might not get the chance to look at an area which you really want to study. There are students who, when asked what area of law interests them, say 'none', the response being to ask why they are doing law in the first place. However, most students do identify better with some areas of law than others and, obviously, will produce better work in those areas than less favoured ones. That said, the lists should have a broad spread to cater for this and to distribute the students round staff, each having students for their particular area of expertise.

If this is the position with your dissertation or extended essay, the procedure for selection should be the same as for an open title, merely within a smaller range of topics. See which areas have plenty of academic debate and focus on those, finding one which meets that criterion and also the one of accessibility – that is, that it is a topic that appeals. If you do this, it should keep you interested throughout the research and writing period and, as a result, bring you the sort of mark that you want.

Above all, whichever category your dissertation or extended essay falls in, make sure that you use the expertise of your tutors in making your choice, and continue to use it throughout the research and writing stages. You will be given parameters within which such supervision is to work but, as long as you stay within those parameters, take full advantage of the assistance available.

Summary

This chapter has discussed:

- how a dissertation or extended essay is unlike a standard assignment;
- how it is more likely to explore an area or test a hypothesis;
- why care needs to be taken in choosing a topic that both appeals you and has a good deal of academic material available;
- how the key to success is to take full advantage of tutor expertise to guide you to your topic area and through to completion.

23 Research Strategies

By the end of this chapter you should be able to:

▶ identify the nature of a law dissertation;
▶ understand the scope of researching an extended work;
▶ identify appropriate sources;
▶ evaluate sources critically.

Defining the dissertation

The first thing to be clear about in looking at research strategies for a law dissertation is what it is not. A law dissertation is not a social science dissertation. The corollary of this is that there should be no place in a law dissertation for primary social science research. Tutors frequently have students who, as part of their dissertation research, say that they want to do a questionnaire, either to distribute within the student cohort or to send to people with a particular interest in the area. Alternatively, they might say that they want to interview people to find their views on the topic area. This is a very bad idea. Firstly, law students have rarely studied social science research methods and so they do not have the expertise to design a questionnaire or structured interview or to analyse the results. Secondly, what use would it be? A student cohort is rarely one which would give statistically significant results, so would be of little use. If the aim is to send it to people outside the university, what incentive would they have to complete it and return it? If the answer is none, as it usually is, they probably will not do so. There is a third reason not to do such research. Generally, law dissertations do not require individual ethical approval before they are undertaken, as they should have group approval based on the dissertation module specification. If you choose to do a survey, both the questionnaire and the sampling method would need individual approval and this would require you to comply with your university's ethics processes, which are normally time-consuming and bureaucratic. Satisfying them would take time which should be better used doing what you should be doing.

This is what a law dissertation is: a literature-based dissertation, relying on primary sources such as statutes and cases and secondary sources such as textbooks, journal articles and other materials, printed and electronic. As a result, your research strategy should be looking at these rather than anything else. Researching these sources is covered in Chapter 4 and what was said there applies even more to dissertations than to standard assignments. If you cannot remember what was said in Chapter 4 (pp. 24–37), go back and read it before coming back here.

The scope of the research

What is specific about researching a dissertation or extended essay as opposed to any other form of assignment? There are two things in particular to bear in mind. The first is that in researching a topic area you will be looking much wider than you will have done for an assignment with a specific question. When you have done this, you will focus on a specific part of the topic for the writing of the work itself. The result will be that there may be significant parts of your research that do not make it into the final article. Do not worry about this; it is part of the learning process. Henry Ford, the head of the Ford Motor Company in the United States, used to say that he knew that half of his advertising budget was wasted but that he did not know which half it was. Similarly here: until you have assembled all the material, you do not know where your focus will be so cannot forecast what will be useful and what will not. It is preferable to go slightly too wide and have too much material than to focus narrowly early on and find when you are writing that material is missing and you have to backtrack to find it.

That said, you still need to be careful to avoid overload. This is particularly true if you are researching an area with vast potential because you need to ensure that the volume you accumulate is manageable; after all, you have to read it. This is where your supervisor can have a real impact, advising you when to restrict your research and when to expand it. However, this is your piece of work so do not expect your supervisor to construct your research strategy for you. What you need to do is to produce a research plan which covers the area that interests you and submit it to your supervisor. That way, your supervisor can advise on narrowing or widening the research with your individual focus in mind. Tutors are often asked by students what would be the best area to concentrate on in a dissertation. The usual answer is: I do not know because it is not my dissertation. The tutor knows what interests them, not what interests the student; and if the student is guided too closely, at what point does the work cease to be the student's own and become the supervisor's? This, probably, will be the piece of work on your degree course that gives you more freedom than any other. Use it. It will pay off in results.

Authority

The second point to make about research strategies is a reinforcement of what was said before rather than an addition. That is, that it is vital in these sorts of assessment to ensure that the sources you are using are authoritative. How you do this is covered in Chapter 4 (pp. 24–37). Citations from newspapers, open access websites or other non-authoritative sources will seriously detract from your work and could cost significantly in marks. No first-class mark will be awarded if these sources are used and even an upper second is unlikely.

Why is this so? The answer is that such a dissertation or extended essay is the culmination of your degree. Although you will probably submit it before your final exams, it should be the peak of your academic achievement. To reach that peak it needs to show that you have not only learned the difference between authoritative sources and others but are able to apply that learning thoroughly and consistently to produce an academic piece of work. If you do not do that you have not met the requirements for it and so will not get top marks. Look at the **learning outcomes** for your course or, if you do not have them, use the ones in Appendix 2 (p. 202). What do they say? The key word here is 'critically' and you cannot be said to have done something critically to a high standard if you have not been capable of discerning which sources are authoritative and which are not.

Sources

Another difference, again in scale, between researching an assignment and researching a dissertation or an extended essay is the balance of your research. When you start in year 1 you will be using textbooks and journal articles in varying proportions depending on the nature of the assignment. As you progress through your course, the balance will change with more references to journal articles and fewer to textbooks. The reason for this is that undergraduate textbooks tend to concentrate on the factual: that is, what the law is, rather than argument. Articles are argument and will give you the critical edge that you need. As you will see in the next chapter, the factual content of a dissertation or extended essay should be quite small and focused in the introduction. Everything else should consist of discussion, argument and particularly the comparing and contrasting of academic authorities. These you are more likely to find in journal articles regardless of whether the journal itself is paper or electronic.

Within a dissertation or extended essay, precisely because of the length of the piece of work compared to normal assignments, there is also more scope to use materials which debate the problem as part of the process of looking for solutions. In particular, Law Commission Consultation Papers are a very good source of such material as they set out the problem being considered very well and proffer options for reform. They tend to be much more analytical than Law Commission Reports, which are about solutions rather than questions. That said, if there is a Law Commission Report on the area you are looking at, make sure you read it. Your university library should have paper copies of these, and those since 1995 are available on the Law Commission's website (www.lawcom.gov.uk) and earlier ones on the British and Irish Legal Information Institute Openlaw website (http://alpha.bailii.org/openlaw/).

Some papers issued by government departments can be useful. However, it is worth being careful with these as, generally, papers are published because the Government is proposing to change something. As a result the papers, particularly Green Papers which are discussion documents and White Papers which are draft reform proposals, can be pushing a particular line and might not be as objective as would be desired.

This problem is even more profound with papers from campaign groups. Obviously, they exist to promote a particular line and so their material is often less than objective. The difficulty here is that not all such groups are open about the line they are pursuing and what can appear to be an objective report can, in truth, be the opposite. Although all the materials you use can have this problem, its effect is minimised by your use of a wide variety of sources. It does not matter that a textbook or journal article is written from a particular standpoint as long as that writer's view is compared and contrasted with opposing views.

This comes back to the issue of how materials become academically authoritative, which was covered in Chapter 4 (p. 26). The further you depart from such sources, the less authoritative will be your work. If you are unsure about a source, ask your supervisor.

Summary

This chapter has made it clear that:

- a law dissertation or extended essay is not a social science work;
- it is a literature-based piece and so research should concentrate on authoritative, academic sources;

- research into these can be wider than for a standard assignment;
- it is vital that non-authoritative materials are not used;
- Law Commission papers are good sources but care needs to be taken with discussion papers and reports from other organisations.

24 Writing the Dissertation or Extended Essay

By the end of this chapter you should be able to:

- ▶ appreciate the value of instructions and the need to follow them;
- ▶ structure an extended work;
- ▶ construct each part;
- ▶ structure conclusions and abstracts.

● The basics

Writing is the important bit as this is what you will be marked on. However, if you have not done the earlier work sufficiently well, you will not be able to write a piece of work that will achieve the marks you want. That said, even if you have done the preparation and research you should have done, it is still easy to throw all that good work away by being careless with the writing up. There are three particular elements which you need to ensure are in place so that you minimise the risks to the project.

The first, and possibly most important, concerns your instructions. If you have been told that the work has to follow a specified format, make sure it does! This may sound so obvious that it should not need saying but tutors are frequently presented with work which does not comply with instructions. This might be as unimportant as not having the correct front sheet to something as important as having been instructed to use a particular structure and then using a different one. So before you start writing, read the instructions again and make sure they are with you whenever you are working on the piece. Although instructions for law dissertations and extended essays tend not to be very prescriptive compared to those in the sciences or social sciences, one thing you almost certainly have is a word limit. *Do not exceed it*: you will be penalised for doing so.

The second element is how the work is written. As this is the culmination of your degree, it needs to be written to the highest possible standard. This was covered in Chapter 6 (p. 53) so, if you cannot remember what was said there, go back and read it again. In particular, recall that adopting a sophisticated approach does not mean using language you do not understand; it means the opposite. For some reason students, in doing these types of assessment, sometimes adopt highly artificial ways of writing, using words inappropriately as they have never done before. The only thing to say about that is: do not do it.

The third element is presentation. Whilst this is probably the least impor-tant of the three, getting it wrong can have a disproportionate effect on the outcome. The reason for this is very simple: tutors are only human and if the work is presented appropriately, using layout, line spacing and fonts as instructed, it is much easier to read than something which is not presented appropriately. As a result, the marker is predisposed in favour of the former and against the latter regardless of content.

Structure

Starting with structure, how should a longer piece of work be designed? Students frequently approach supervisors with plans for multiple chapters, often as many as ten. Given that undergraduate word limits are normally up to 15,000 words, a ten-chapter piece would be a series of short items rather than a whole. Although there is no magic number of sections you ought to have, there is a minimum and that is three. If your extended essay is only 5000 words that will often be the right number because it encompasses an introduction, the main discussion and a conclusion. In a 5000-word piece these are likely to be sections of the work rather than separate chapters, whereas in longer pieces they almost certainly would be chapters.

If you have 10,000 to 15,000 words to play with, the introduction and conclusion remain, but it is sensible to break the discussion up into its component parts, always remembering that this is a coherent piece of work not a set of small ones, but you still need to be fairly sparing with how you do it. Again, there is no magic number but, as a guide, it would be sensible for a 10,000-word piece not to exceed five chapters including the introduc-tion and conclusion, as an absolute limit, and a 15,000-word piece to have no more than seven. In each case, fewer would probably be better, say four chapters for the 10,000-word one and five or six for 15,000 words.

Starting with the introduction, this should be the only factual part of the work and, in view of this, should be fairly short. What you are doing is setting out what the task is, what is the problem you are discussing and why. In Chapter 10 it was said that the definitional part of an essay should be no more than 10 per cent and that would be a starting point here. As you have more space to play with and something more complex to define, you may need to go above 10 per cent for your introduction but you should consider 15 per cent to be an absolute limit and use a lower figure if possible. For a 10,000-word piece, that means that your introduction should be limited to 1000–1500 words and for a 15,000 word one, 1500–2250. As with essays, conclusions should aim for about half these figures, so a conclusion of

500–750 words for a 10,000-word piece and 750–1125 for a 15,000-word one. If you obey these rules it will mean that the main body will be about 80 per cent of it, giving you the scope to develop your argument.

Although the differences between a dissertation or extended essay and a standard essay have been noted as the exploration of an idea or hypothesis as opposed to answering a specific question, the similarities need to be noted too. The key element in writing is that you stick to your topic, and to the narrowed focus which your research has produced. In order to do this, you need a plan for what you are going to do before you start. Your research should have produced a number of strands to the problem or argument and, in narrowing to a focus, this should have left you with a limited number of areas you are going to explore within the overall topic. These are your chapters. If you have too many areas, you are still too wide and you need to narrow further until you get to the right number. As an introduction and a conclusion have already been specified, this leaves you looking at two or three areas for a 10,000-word piece or three to five areas for a 15,000-word one.

Construction

Your research will have produced a set of subsections, as each writer has discussed the area you are going to cover in a chapter. This will give you the spine of the chapter just as was done in the earlier examples of assessment. This spine is then filled out with the detail of each writer's views, remembering to compare and contrast their individual points rather than merely stating what they are. This fills out the spine into a chapter. Do not try to plan the whole work like this beforehand or you will never start writing. Plan your introduction and write it. Then plan the second chapter and write that and so on. Again, ideas will occur to you as you are writing for ways to vary what you have planned. This is fine; it shows you are still thinking through the area and learning from what you are doing. However, as with other sorts of assessment, do not follow the idea thinking that you will return to the structure eventually. Amend the structure to take account of the variation so that you still have a functioning structure in front of you.

In order that each chapter works, both internally to itself and as a component of the whole piece, it needs to be coherent. Just as with paragraphs in other assessments, the chapter should start with a definition of what is to be covered. As you have set out the problem in your introduction, subsequent chapters can refer back to this so that you are not repeating what you have already said or making chapters other than the introduction factual. Similarly, each chapter should draw the argument it has conducted to a conclusion so that when you get to the conclusion of the work, what you are doing is drawing together the conclusions of the various chapters.

The main part of each chapter will consist of the subsections of the argument as you have identified them in your research. To subdivide these into paragraph-length parts it is sometimes easiest to analyse one writer or school of thought at a time, using the subsequent paragraph to put a contrasting or comparable view. This needs discipline since it is easy to let this run on into a set of listings: if one paragraph is of one author make sure the next one is not. This, rather than comparing or contrasting within a paragraph, will give you the space to explore the question at the depth necessary for this type of work. As with essays, your footnote references should be a clue as to whether you are doing it correctly or not. A set of references to one source followed by a set of references to another source suggests too much of a list and insufficient comparing and contrasting. It is important that your paragraphs do not become massive slabs of text. If this happens, split the subsection into two parts, cover each part separately and draw a mini-conclusion after the second part.

Once a chapter has been done, do not be afraid to revise it – particularly if a subsequent chapter shows there is something missing. However, obey the rules when you are doing it: so revise within an amended plan rather than freestyle tinkering. When you have revised and are comfortable with the result, leave that chapter alone and move on. Students frequently say that they just want to do something or other to a chapter that they had finished and revised. If you keep doing that you will never finish because there is always something else that could be done. It is also common that students will tinker with something and, in doing so, lose the coherence the piece originally had.

Once the main body of the work is completed, you can use conclusions from each chapter to draw the work to an overall conclusion. What is important here is that it is a conclusion, summarising the discussion which has preceded it. This should mean that you do not introduce anything into the conclusion that has not been covered in the work itself. If something has been covered, refer back to it; if it has not, then exclude it. A new reference in a conclusion is a depressing sight because it means the student has not structured their material well enough to include it. If it is that vital, you can always go back and revise the relevant chapter.

Additional items

Once you have written your conclusion you will know what the work is about and you can do the final two substantive things which you need for a major piece of work: a title and an abstract. Obviously you have had a working topic throughout but as the focus has narrowed, this will have become too wide. Narrow this back down to reflect accurately what you have written and the title will look as though it belongs with the piece.

Abstracts are fairly straightforward but, in undergraduate work, tend to be done badly. There is a simple reason for this: it is the first abstract you have ever written. The result is that most abstracts in undergraduate work actually read as introductions. An abstract does not say what a piece of work is going to say; it says what it has said. From the abstract the reader should be able to get a fair idea of what has been covered by the piece, including the conclusion, to gauge if it is what they are looking for. Abstracts should never exceed one side of paper at the same line spacing and font as the main work. This would suggest 350 words as a maximum and fewer if possible.

Once you have a piece of work that is in more than one part, a contents page is useful, giving a page number for each chapter. Make sure it also includes the abstract and bibliography.

In constructing the bibliography, as specified in Chapter 6 (p. 68), make sure it reflects the work as it has been written rather than being a list of everything that is possibly relevant. If you have not used a particular source in the work itself, do not include it in the bibliography. As you have excluded some of your research in narrowing your topic to the size available to you, exclude it from the bibliography. It may be a useful source but it is a source for the work you did *not* write, not for the one you did. If you cram everything in, the marker is entitled to ask: where did that go?

It is normal with such a piece that acknowledgement is made of those who helped or made the piece possible. This should include your supervisor and any other member of staff who has advised you on any part of it. Although it is acceptable here to acknowledge the contribution made by others who have enabled you to complete your degree, the acknowledgement should be to thank them rather than being something particularly effusive.

Finally, do not wait until submission day to print your dissertation or extended essay – something is bound to go wrong. Crying down the phone to your supervisor half an hour before the deadline that your printer has gone wrong is unlikely to evoke much sympathy. If possible, get it printed a week before submission day; if that is not possible do it at least 3 days before, and if you are required to submit the dissertation bound, allow time for that process too. This will ensure that, when the day comes, you can hand it in early. Then it is out of the way and you can think about revising for your final exams in the knowledge that one of the major components of your degree has been done.

Summary

In this chapter we have shown that:

- the keys to writing a dissertation or extended essay are structure, the standard of writing and presentation;
- the structure needs to limit the factual to the introduction and leave chapters of appropriate length for argument and analysis;
- the chapters should be constructed with a spine drawn from the research, filled out with the views of the writers considered;
- each chapter should conclude and these conclusions be drawn together for a conclusion to the work as a whole;
- a title, abstract and acknowledgements should complete the work.

Appendix 1: University Marking and Assessment Criteria

● **Marking Criteria**

Level 1

90%–100%
Excellent work with presentation of a very high standard. There is coherence of ideas and demonstration of a thorough knowledge and understanding. Arguments are supported by wide reading with very effective use of source material and accurate referencing.

80%–89%
Outstanding work with presentation of a very high standard. There is coherence of ideas and demonstration of a thorough knowledge and understanding. Arguments are supported by wide reading with effective use of source material and accurate referencing.

70%–79%
Extremely good work with presentation of a high standard. There is coherence of ideas and demonstration of thorough knowledge and understanding. Arguments are supported by wide reading with appropriate use of source material and accurate referencing.

60%–69%
The work is well presented and coherently structured. There is evidence of a sound knowledge and understanding of the issues with theory linked to practice where appropriate. Most material used has been referenced/acknowledged.

50%–59%
Presentation is acceptable but with some errors. There is knowledge and understanding of issues under discussion and some evidence of the application of knowledge and ideas where appropriate. Some use of relevant source material.

40%–49%
Presentation is acceptable but attention to structure, style and referencing is required. The content is relevant but largely descriptive. There is evidence of a reasonable level of knowledge and understanding, sufficient to meet the

learning outcomes, but there is limited use of source material to support the arguments, proposals or solutions. Some links are made to practice where appropriate.

35%–39% – borderline fail
The presentation is acceptable but requires considerable attention to style, structure, grammar and referencing. The level of knowledge and understanding displayed is sufficient to meet most of the learning outcomes, but not all. There is limited use of source material to support the work presented, the work is very descriptive and lacks any evidence of analysis.

30%–34% – fail
The work is poorly structured and presented. Some material may be irrelevant. Content is based largely on taught elements with very little evidence of reading around the topic and little or no reference to practice where appropriate. The learning outcomes are not met.

29% and below – fail
The work is very poorly structured and presented. Much material is irrelevant. Content is based almost entirely on taught elements with very little evidence of any purposeful reading around the topic. No effective reference to practice where appropriate. The learning outcomes are not met. To attain 20% the work must show evidence of a genuine attempt to demonstrate some knowledge of the subject.

< 20% – fail
The work is virtually entirely derivative and fails to demonstrate understanding or knowledge of issues. The presentation and referencing does not conform to expected standards.

Level 2

90%–100%
Excellent work with presentation of the highest standard. The work contains coherent arguments and ideas. There is a detailed understanding of subject matter and critical analysis of issues/problems. Points are made clearly and concisely, always substantiated by appropriate use of source material. There is evidence of a sound ability to critically interrelate theories with examples from practice where appropriate.

80%–89%
Outstanding work with presentation of a very high standard. There is comprehensive understanding of key concepts and knowledge and evidence of critical analysis and insight. Accurate interpretation of data with arguments, ideas and solutions presented effectively and based on strong research and reading.

70%–79%
Extremely good work with presentation of a high standard. Evidence of strong knowledge and understanding together with some critical analysis and

insight. Source material is used effectively to support arguments, ideas and solutions.

60%–69%
Very good presentation. Sound knowledge and understanding with an emerging ability to critically engage with and apply the concepts involved, linking them to practice where appropriate. Good use of source material, which supports most points clearly. Content is wholly relevant and is coherently structured.

50%–59%
Presentation is of a good standard but with some shortcomings. Evidence of a sound knowledge base but limited critical and practical application of concepts and ideas. Content is largely relevant although points may not always be clear and structure may lack coherence. Contains some critical reflection and some use of source material to illustrate points.

40%–49%
Adequate presentation. The work is descriptive and/or lacks critical analysis where required but is relevant with limited though sufficient evidence of knowledge and understanding. There is some evidence of reading although arguments/proposals/solutions often lack coherence and may be unsubstantiated by relevant source material or partially flawed. Links to practice are made where appropriate.

35%–39% – borderline fail
Most of the above, but not all the learning outcomes are met, and the work demonstrates a weak knowledge base and non-compliance with the School requirements for referencing.

30%–34% – fail
Poorly structured, incoherent and wholly descriptive work. Evidence of a weak knowledge base with some key aspects not addressed and use of irrelevant material. Learning outcomes are not met. Flawed use of techniques. Limited evidence of appropriate reading and no evidence of critical thought. Little reference to practice where appropriate.

29% and below – fail
Learning outcomes not met. Very poorly structured, incoherent and wholly descriptive work. Evidence of a very weak knowledge base with many key omissions and much material irrelevant. Use of inappropriate or incorrect techniques. Limited evidence of appropriate reading and no evidence of critical thought. No links to practice where appropriate. To obtain 20% the work must show evidence of a genuine attempt to demonstrate some knowledge of the subject.

< 20% – fail
The work is almost entirely derivative and therefore lacks analysis or reflection, and shows little knowledge or understanding of issues. The presentation and referencing does not conform to the standards required by the School.

Level 3

90%–100%
Exceptional work. Presentation is logical, error-free and, where appropriate, creative. There is an in-depth understanding of issues/problems and excellent critical/deep engagement with the material and concepts involved. Very skilful interpretation of data. Arguments, ideas and, where appropriate, solutions are presented coherently and fully underpinned by thorough research and reading. The referencing is impeccable.

80%–89%
Outstanding work with presentation of a very high standard. There is comprehensive understanding of key concepts and knowledge and clear evidence of critical analysis and insight. Accurate interpretation of data with arguments, ideas and solutions presented effectively and based on strong research and reading, with excellent use of referencing.

70%–79%
Extremely good work with presentation of a high standard. Demonstrates an excellent knowledge base with a clear understanding of the issues and application to practice where appropriate. There is some effective critical and analytical application of relevant research and reading. The referencing is of high standard and conforms to School standards.

60%–69%
The work is very good, logically structured and presented to a high standard. Demonstrates a strong knowledge base with a clear understanding of the issues and application to practice where appropriate. There is some critical and analytical application of relevant research. Referencing is of high standard but minor errors are evident.

50%–59%
The work is clearly presented and logically structured. It shows evidence of a sound understanding of the topic and addresses major issues. The work contains some discussion and interpretation of relevant perspectives although further development of the arguments presented would be beneficial. There are examples of critical reflection and evidence of application of theory to practice. Referencing conforms largely to the School standards and style.

40%–49%
Adequate presentation. The work displays basic knowledge and understanding of the topic sufficient to meet the learning outcomes, but is largely descriptive. There is an attempt to bring together different ideas and concepts although this would have been strengthened by the inclusion of further key issues. The structure of the work requires attention to its coherence and logical development of content. The link between theory and practice, where appropriate, is somewhat tenuous and its development would enhance the

work considerably. Referencing does not fully conform to the School standards and style.

35%–39% – borderline fail
Adequate presentation, with a weak but basic knowledge and understanding that meets some but not all of the learning outcomes. Evidence of application of theory to the issues is weak, and the work contains numerous unsupported statements, a poor structure and limited critical analysis.

30%–34% – fail
The work is poorly presented and contains numerous errors, inconsistencies and omissions with limited use of source material. The work displays a weak knowledge base and lack of sufficient understanding of the topic. The learning outcomes are not met. There is little or no evidence of the application of theory to practice where appropriate. It contains many unsupported statements with little attempt to bring issues together and lacks critical analysis and reflection.

29% and below – fail
The work is very poorly presented and contains numerous serious errors, inconsistencies and omissions with little use of source material. The work displays a very weak knowledge base and a lack of sufficient understanding of the topic. There is little or no evidence of the application of theory to practice where appropriate. It contains many unsupported statements with little attempt to bring issues together and there is a complete lack of critical analysis and reflection. Referencing is of poor standard. To obtain 20% the work must show evidence of a genuine attempt to demonstrate some knowledge of the subject.

< 20% – fail
The work is largely derivative and therefore lacks analysis or reflection, and shows little knowledge or understanding of issues. The presentation and referencing does not conform to the standards required by the School.

Assessment Criteria for Presentations

Name(s): 1
2

	Fail	40–49	50–59	60–69	70+	Mark
1 Did the students introduce themselves?	No	Basic			Appropriately	
2 Were they dressed appropriately?	No	Some effort made	Moderately well	Quite well	Appropriately	
3 Speech – volume	Inaudible	Difficult to hear/ shouting	Moderately easy	Quite easy to hear	Totally suitable	
4 Speech – pace	So fast as to be unintelligible	Too fast and stumbled over words	A little fast/ slow	Quite appropriately paced	Paced well	
5 Speech – intonation	No intonation	Some variations in tone	Moderately varied tone	Quite well varied in tone	Very well intoned	
6 Body language	No movement	Some movement	Moderately appropriate	Good standard	Excellent standard	
7 Eye contact	No eye contact	Some eye contact	Engaged moderately	Good standard	Excellent use	
8 Reading from script	Reading badly	Reading but intelligible	Mostly reading but some departure	Some reading but engaged well	Reference to notes but not reading	
9 Use of aids	Unsatisfactory/ none	Fairly disordered	Reasonably well	Good standard	Excellent standard	
10 Overall impression						

Assessment Criteria for Moots

Name(s): 1
2

	Fail	40–49	50–59	60–69	70+	Mark
1 Did the students introduce themselves?	No	Basic			Appropriately	
2 Were they dressed appropriately?	No	Some effort made	Moderately well	Quite well	Appropriately	
3 Speech – volume	Inaudible	Difficult to hear/shouting	Moderately easy	Quite easy to hear	Totally suitable	
4 Speech – pace	So fast as to be unintelligible	Too fast and stumbled over words	A little fast/slow	Quite appropriately paced	Paced well	
5 Speech – intonation	No intonation	Some variations in tone	Moderately varied tone	Quite well varied in tone	Very well intoned	
6 Body language and eye contact	No movement or eye contact	Some movement and some eye contact	Moderately appropriate	Good standard	Excellent standard	
7 Reading from script	Reading badly	Reading but intelligible	Mostly reading but some departure	Some reading but engaged well	Reference to notes but not reading	

8 Use of skeleton argument	Did not use	Some use	Moderate use	Used well and appropriately	Excellent use
9 Use of case law/statute/other items	Unsatisfactory	Some use of case law	Moderate use of cases	Cases used well and appropriately	Excellent use
10 Order of case law	Unsatisfactory	Fairly disordered	Reasonably well ordered	Good standard	Excellent standard
11 Did they address the court correctly?	No address/totally inappropriate	Some address	Reasonable address	Good standard	Totally appropriate
12 Overall impression					

Assessment Criteria for Poster Presentations

Name:

Did the student:	Fail	40–49	50–59	60–69	70+	Mark
1 Access information from a range of sources?	No sources identified	Basic			Very wide	
2 Distinguish primary and secondary sources?	No clear distinction	Primary sources indentified	Primary and secondary sources indentified and ranked	Identification of conflict between sources with a class	Very fine distinctions between conflicting authorities and a balance of secondary sources	
3 Select and critically evaluate relevant information from sources?	No relevant material identified	Relevant material identified	Relevant material identified and attempt to evaluate material	Identification and good evaluation of material	Excellent identification and evaluation of material	
4 Formulate appropriate question?	No question	A question that does not naturally flow from material	A question that flows from the material but may	The question flows from the material and would lend	A question that flows from the material and	

		presented	need refining	itself to a research project	demonstrates clear understanding of the issues
5 Formulate appropriate methodology to address the question?	No method of completing the project considered	The method is there but not clearly identified	The method is explained but not entirely appropriate for resources, time etc.	The method is clear and appropriate to the question and resources	The method is clear, appropriate and demonstrates some originality
6 Present information in an appropriate manner?	Poor presentation inappropriate to the task	Acceptable standard of presentation demonstrating basic skills	Good standard of presentation appropriate to material, some errors but shows relevant skills	Good standard of presentation appropriate to material, few errors and range of relevant skills	Excellent standard of presentation, wholly appropriate, demonstrating a wide range of skills
7 Overall impression					

Appendix 2: Learning Outcomes

● **LLB Single Honours: Stage Outcomes**

Level 1

Knowledge and understanding

1.1   Describe and explain the nature and development of English law and the English legal system.

1.2   Identify and explain basic principles relevant to contractual obligations and criminal liability.

1.3   Identify and explain the moral and social principles that underpin the law.

1.4   Explain the interaction between common law and statute.

1.5   Describe and explain the nature of the constitution.

1.6   Explain the significance of the European Convention on Human Rights and the Human Rights Act 1998.

Cognitive and intellectual skills

1.7   Identify legal issues and apply relevant legal principles to arrive at justifiable solutions to legal problems, real or hypothetical, of limited complexity.

1.8   Identify and distinguish between primary and secondary sources, with guidance, relevant to the given task.

1.9   Discriminate between legally relevant and irrelevant information.

Practical and professional skills

1.10 Bring together relevant materials, with guidance, from a range of sources in preparation for tutorial exercises and assignments.

1.11 Use legal terminology appropriately.

Key transferable skills

1.12 Carry out instructions effectively.

1.13 Manage time efficiently, with guidance, in order to meet deadlines.

1.14 Begin to appreciate personal strengths and weaknesses, reflect on quality of understanding and recognise when to seek and how to use feedback.

1.15 Cooperate and work with peers to prepare tutorials and moots.

1.16 Communicate appropriately in group discussion in tutorials.

1.17 Undertake an internet search.

1.18 Use electronic communication effectively.

1.19 Use basic IT tools for word processing (Word) and Presentation (PowerPoint).

1.20 Write clearly and concisely using legal conventions.

1.21 Communicate appropriately in speech using basic advocacy skills.

Level 2

Knowledge and understanding

2.1 Demonstrate a detailed knowledge of principles of the substantive areas of law studied at this level.

2.2 Critically analyse current law, both statute and common law, and proposals for reform.

Cognitive and intellectual skills

2.3 Employ balanced and logical argument to arrive at justifiable solutions to legal problems of greater complexity.

2.4 Critically analyse abstract legal concepts.

2.5 Critically examine law in its social and political context.

2.6 Evaluate the effectiveness of substantive law in selected areas.

2.7 Critically analyse inconsistent lines of precedent or differing interpretations of statutory provisions.

2.8 Identify issues of difficulty requiring further research and select appropriate tools and methods to arrive at solutions.

2.9 Critically evaluate opinions of legal commentators.

2.10 Critically review methods of collecting and presenting (e.g. statistically) empirical data.

Practical and professional skills

2.11 Select and rank relevant information from a wide range of sources including important professional electronic databases (LexisNexis and Westlaw).

2.12 Explore ethical issues relevant to research.

2.13 Undertake appropriate research for tutorial and assignment preparation with limited guidance.

Key transferable skills

2.14 Organise group work, assigning tasks/roles where necessary.

2.15 Select means of communication/presentation appropriate to the task.

2.16 Employ balanced and logical argument in oral discussion.

2.17 Reflect systematically on own learning.

2.18 Review career aspirations.

2.19 Work with reduced class contact time.

Level 3

Knowledge and understanding

3.1 Synthesise and critically appraise the principles governing certain areas of substantive law (selected by the student and studied in depth) in their social, economic, historical, commercial or political context as appropriate.

3.2 Demonstrate a comprehensive knowledge and deep understanding of a legal issue chosen, analysed, researched and presented by the student as a dissertation.

Cognitive and intellectual skills

3.3 Employ open-minded, logical and balanced argument to arrive at justifiable solutions to complex legal problems.

3.4 Synthesise, appraise and evaluate information from appropriate sources.

3.5 Critically review legal developments, expose limitations in current legal provisions and, where appropriate, make recommendations for reform.

Practical and professional skills

3.6 Undertake independent research in topics negotiated with tutors.

3.7 Be proactive in discovering and using sources of law.

Key transferable skills

3.8 Plan, manage and evaluate own approach to learning.

3.9 Communicate clearly, fluently and effectively in writing in a manner appropriate to the context using appropriate aids, IT packages, etc.

3.10 Present academic argument orally and engage in discussion of those arguments effectively.

3.11 Employ numeracy skills where appropriate.

LLB Single Honours: Dissertation Outcomes

Knowledge and understanding
1. Demonstrate a comprehensive and detailed knowledge of the dissertation topic in appropriate contexts.

Cognitive and intellectual skills
2. Synthesise and critically appraise different aspects of the issues under consideration.

Practical and professional skills
3. Apply skills of research using methodologies acquired earlier and, in particular, identify and retrieve sources with a minimal need for guidance.
4. Identify and define complex legal problems and apply legal principles to arrive at a structured written presentation.

Key transferable skills
5. Communicate clearly, fluently and effectively.
6. Act autonomously with limited supervision or direction within agreed guidelines.

● **LLB Single Honours: Poster Presentation Outcomes**

You must prepare an individual poster presentation of a dissertation proposal on a topic selected of your choice. This topic could be the topic you wish to choose for your final-year dissertation.

Before putting together your poster, consider the learning outcomes for the module – the poster is the means of assessing whether or not these are achieved.

Main Learning Outcomes

On successful completion of this module, the student will:

1. Appreciate the nature of the research process and be aware of the research methodologies used by lawyers and other disciplines.
2. Critically examine selected topics and identify areas of controversy or conflict.
3. Evaluate specific pressures/proposals for change including the validity of relevant precursor research, and assess the implications of these proposals/pressures.
4. Formulate appropriate questions for further research and a methodology to address these questions.
5. Access and select relevant information from a wide range of sources including legal-specific online databases.
6. Appreciate the nature of research ethics.
7. Present information in an appropriate manner.

The vehicle for assessing whether or not you have met these outcomes is the poster. See the Poster Presentation marking criteria in Appendix 1. These are the criteria that will be used to assess each poster but try not to be too mechanical in your approach to them; different topics will require emphasis to be placed in different areas and there is room for you to be creative in your interpretation of them.

Appendix 3: Case Citations

Neutral Citations

These are citations provided by the courts that do not depend on the source of the Report.

UKSC	United Kingdom Supreme Court
UKHL	United Kingdom House of Lords (to 2009)
UKPC	United Kingdom Privy Council
EWCA Civ	England and Wales Court of Appeal, Civil Division
EWCA Crim	England and Wales Court of Appeal, Criminal Division
EWHC (Admin)	England and Wales High Court, Administrative Court
EWHC (Ch)	England and Wales High Court, Chancery Division
EWHC (Comm)	England and Wales High Court, Commercial Court
EWHC (Fam)	England and Wales High Court, Family Division
EWHC (QB)	England and Wales High Court, Queen's Bench Division
EWHC (TCC)	England and Wales High Court, Technology and Construction Court

Law Reports

These are citations for particular sets of Law Reports and are different in each set. There are a large number of these so only the most common are given.

All ER	All England Law Reports
AC	Law Reports, Appeal Cases
Ch	Law Reports, Chancery
Cr App R	Criminal Appeal Reports
Fam	Law Reports, Family
KB	Law Reports, King's Bench
Lloyd's Rep	Lloyd's Law Reports
Med LR	Medical Law Reports
QB	Law Reports, Queen's Bench
WLR	Weekly Law Reports

Glossary

Note: where a term from the Glossary appears in the main text it is printed in **bold**.

Academic stage The academic law course which those intending to become solicitors or barristers must complete before beginning their professional training. This is normally either an undergraduate law degree or a law conversion course such as a Graduate Diploma or Postgraduate Diploma.

Appellant The party to a case who appeals against a lower court decision.

Appellate courts These are courts which hear appeals from the decisions of lower courts. In English law this generally means the Supreme Court from October 2009 (and up to 2009, the House of Lords) and the Court of Appeal, both by its Civil Division and its Criminal Division. The High Court does have some appellate jurisdiction over the Crown Court but this is limited and there are proposals for it to be abolished.

Bar Professional Training Course This is the successor to the earlier Bar Vocational Course and is the course which those intending to become barristers must complete after the academic stage of their training and before taking a pupillage.

Claimant The person bringing a civil court action.

Defendant The person against whom an action is brought in either a civil or criminal court.

Dissenting judgment The judgment given by a judge or judges in a court where the case is decided by more than one judge, which disagrees with the decision of the majority.

Equity	The body of principles which grew from the decisions of Lords Chancellor and later the Court of Chancery.
Learning outcomes	The results of student learning which are to be measured for a form of assessment, subject, course stage or course.
Legal Practice Course	This is the course which those who intend to be solicitors must complete after the academic stage of training and before entering a training contract.
Marking criteria	These are sets of provisions which detail where a mark is set for a piece of assessed work.
Plaintiff	Until the reforms of 2000 this was the name given to the person who brought an action in a civil court.
Professional courses	The Legal Practice Course and Bar Professional Training Course
Respondent	The party to a case against whom the appellant is appealing. In older cases it was the term used for a party against whom a civil law claim was being made.
VLE	Virtual Learning Environment. This is a term used to describe computer-based systems that provide learning support to students. They may be systems a university has bought the use of, such as Blackboard, Moodle and WebCT, or the university's own system, normally an intranet.

Bibliography

Askey, Simon, and Ian McLeod. *Studying Law*, 2nd edn. Basingstoke: Palgrave Macmillan, 2008.

Finch, Emily, and Stefan Fafinski. *Legal Skills*, 2nd edn. Oxford: Oxford University Press, 2009.

Hill, Jeffrey. *A Practical Guide to Mooting*. Basingstoke: Palgrave Macmillan, 2009.

Holland, James, and Julian Webb. *Learning Legal Rules*, 7th edn. Oxford: Oxford University Press, 2010.

McLeod, Ian. *Key Concepts in Law*, 2nd edn. Basingstoke: Palgrave Macmillan, 2010.

McLeod, Ian. *Legal Method*, 7th edn. Basingstoke: Palgrave Macmillan, 2009.

Ward, Richard, and Amanda Akhtar. *Walker & Walker's English Legal System*, 10th edn. Oxford: Oxford University Press, 2008.

Index